The Little Aussie Fact Book

The Little Aussie Fact Book

Margaret Nicholson

Pitman

Melbourne   London   Toronto   Wellington

PITMAN PUBLISHING
A division of Longman Cheshire Pty Ltd
Kings Gardens, 95 Coventry Street,
Melbourne 3205 Australia
Offices in Sydney, Brisbane,
Adelaide and Perth

First published 1985
Fourth edition 1988

Designed by Lynda Patullo
Illustrations by Mark Patullo and Geoff Kelly
Set in Helvetica
Printed in Hong Kong

National Library of Australia
Cataloguing in Publication data

   Nicholson, Margaret.
   The little Aussie fact book 88.

   4th ed.
   Bibliography
   ISBN 0 7299 0124 6

   1 Australia, Miscellanea. 1. Title.
994

Contents

Breathes there the man, with soul so dead,
Who never to himself hath said,
'This is my own, my native land!'
                                    Sir Walter Scott

Preface

I am pleased to present this new edition of the Little Aussie Fact Book. Since the first edition was published in 1985, many readers have expressed their pleasure at the help it has given them in recalling facts long forgotten, or in discovering new facts about our wonderful country. This is very satisfying for me as I set about writing the book when I realised that there was a great need for a compact ready reference book about Australia.

My research led me to explore many facets of Australian culture, history and political structure which are not generally well known. At every step along the way, I was both surprised and intrigued by what I was discovering.

It was not my intention to provide exhaustive information on all aspects of Australia, but rather to combine essential and

practical information in a condensed form which I hope will appeal to the average person. I have also tried to make this book as visual as possible for quick reference, and have attempted at all times to obtain the latest information.

This book has proven to be of help to the visitor or new settler to the country, as well as to the Aussie, both at home and abroad, who finds it difficult to remember the words to songs or answers to the inevitable questions asked about Australia.

A sense of belonging plays an important part in the emotional make-up of most people and perhaps my overriding hope when I considered writing this book was to encourage Australians to be more aware of the background and heritage of this land to which we belong.

Margaret Nicholson 1988

Past

Prehistory

During the ice-age, perhaps as early as 70 000 years ago, peoples and animals of the northern hemisphere began to drift southwards to escape the intense, advancing cold, as well as to find new food supplies. As a result, more southerly groups were pushed even further south, causing a chain reaction of migration.

The ice had built up in the waters of the sea to form massive ice caps, lowering the level of the water (estimated to be 70–90 metres lower than it is today). This uncovered bridges between land masses, nearly joining islands and making migration possible. People in crude craft were able to 'island hop' and perhaps it was possible for the first human inhabitants of Australia unknowingly to enter the great southern continent.

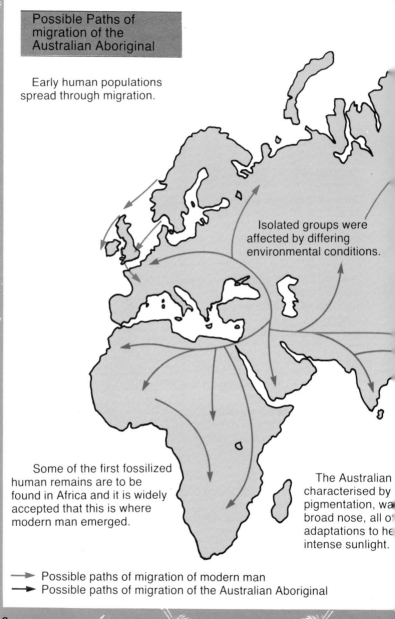

Possible Paths of migration of the Australian Aboriginal

Early human populations spread through migration.

Isolated groups were affected by differing environmental conditions.

Some of the first fossilized human remains are to be found in Africa and it is widely accepted that this is where modern man emerged.

The Australian characterised by pigmentation, wa broad nose, all o adaptations to he intense sunlight.

→ Possible paths of migration of modern man
→ Possible paths of migration of the Australian Aboriginal

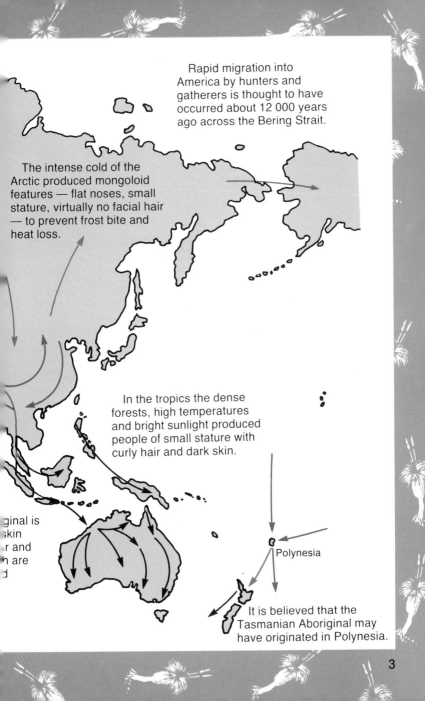

Rapid migration into America by hunters and gatherers is thought to have occurred about 12 000 years ago across the Bering Strait.

The intense cold of the Arctic produced mongoloid features — flat noses, small stature, virtually no facial hair — to prevent frost bite and heat loss.

In the tropics the dense forests, high temperatures and bright sunlight produced people of small stature with curly hair and dark skin.

...ginal is
...skin
...r and
...n are
...d

Polynesia

It is believed that the Tasmanian Aboriginal may have originated in Polynesia.

3

Aboriginal history

Some Aboriginal tribal regions

Tiwi
Larrakia Yoingu
Mildjingi
Dalabon Guma
Kakadu
Ingaladdi Larg
Wandjina
Nyulnyul
Warramanga
Gurindji
Kalkadoor
Karadjeri Walbiri
Pintubi
Wilgie Mia Wenamba Aranda
Pitjantjatjara Matuntara
Dieri
Nakako
Wongkongur
Wirangu
Kaurna
Whadjuk

Archaeological sites found

● More than 30 000 years old
III 15 000–30 000 years old
◎ 10 000–15 000 years old

Then and Now

In my dreams I hear my tribe
Laughing as they hunt and swim,
But dreams are shattered by
    rushing car,
By grinding tram and hissing train,
And I see no more my tribe of old
As I walk alone in the teeming
    town.

I have seen corroboree
Where that factory belches smoke;
Here where they have memorial
    park
One time lubras dug for yams;
One time our dark children played
There where the railway yards are
    now,
And where I remember the
    didgeridoo
Calling to us to dance and play,
Offices now, neon lights now,
Bank and shop and advertisement
    now,
Traffic and trade of the busy town.
No more woomera, no more
    boomerang,
No more playabout, no more the
    old ways.
Children of nature we were then,
No clocks hurrying crowds to toil.
Now I am civilized and work in the
    white way,
Now I have dress, now I have
    shoes:
'Isn't she lucky to have a good
    job!'
Better when I had only a dillybag.
Better when I had nothing but
    happiness.

KATH WALKER

5

Aboriginal culture

The Australian Aboriginal existed in almost total isolation from the rest of mankind for well over 40 000 years. They had no written history, so we now only have fragments of Dreamtime stories, cave paintings and rock etchings to record their remarkable past. It is only in the last few decades that systematic investigation has revealed the rich and complex culture that they surely possessed.

Theirs was and still is a culture based on a deep and strong spiritual life and traditions which link them inexorably to the ancient land around them. Traditionally, it is believed that the land was a gift from the Creator of the Dreamtime. Tradition also teaches that people are born of the spirit which inhabits the land and that on dying they will return to the soil to be born again. Each person is thought to be descended from something in Nature, such as a plant or an animal, and this becomes their 'totem'. Each totem has its own taboos or rules of behaviour.

Before white settlement, the Aboriginals were a very diverse people occupying most of the continent. They spoke many languages and had differing technologies.

Their spiritual and cultural traditions varied, but because of their mutual sense of unity with the land and creation, they existed in comparative harmony.

There were about 600 Aboriginal tribes on the Australian mainland before European contact. A tribe was a group of people related by actual or implied genealogy, speaking a common language and occupying a recognised tract of land over which they hunted and gathered food. The tribes were subdivided by kinship, into clans. Each group lived within its own tribal boundaries which they believed were allocated in the Dreamtime. Each tribe was responsible for the protection and maintenance of sacred sites within their territory and outsiders visited only by invitation. Trade and ceremonial activities allowed borders to be crossed and it is significant that there is no evidence of one tribe coveting another's land.

The tribes had no chiefs, only tribal elders who, because of their experience and wisdom, were considered suitable for making decisions and upholding the laws. Proper behaviour was demanded for every occasion and breaches of law brought severe penalties.

The economy was based on

the relentless, daily activities of hunting, gathering seeds and fishing. Hunting, which was carried out in strict silence, was considered to be 'men's' work, while the collecting of seeds was left to the women. Scarcity of food and water caused by drought, was interpreted to mean that the spirit world was displeased and that 'man must make amends'. Both the men and the women made and repaired tools. Spears, boomerangs, shields, digging sticks were made of wood, but the Aboriginals were also highly skilled at shaping stone implements. They started using ground-edge tools about 10 000 years before their European counterparts.

Aboriginal society was a creative one and art, music, song and dance were integrated into both daily routine and spiritual ritual. The elders prescribed the spiritual form of ceremonial life, particularly in the initiation, marriage, and burial rituals. The rest of the tribe was also totally involved, with prominent roles being taken by the songmen and artists. All around were visible signs of the spirit world. Corroborees and cave paintings reflected the powers of the Dreamtime. Symbolic designs linking the Aboriginals to the land were etched into most objects: from the most insignificant tool to the most sacred Dreamtime stone, the Tjurunga, (see page 110).

Sorcery was not a daily occurrence although no one doubted its power. 'Pointing the bone' the most dreaded magic used by sorcerers, projected the power of evil hidden in the bone into the victim's body.

As the Aboriginal confronted European settlers the whole fabric of this fragile society was shaken. Early contact was usually made on the outskirts of towns where the materialistic values of the white man clashed with the traditionally co-operative sharing of the Aboriginal. Frontiers were eroded and the Aboriginies, separated from their spirit place and stable environment, found that they had nowhere to go.

Aboriginal children

The Intrepid Explorers

'No country can possibly have a more interesting aspect . . . if a further trace into the interior is required . . . I respectfully beg leave to offer myself for the service. I see no end to travelling'. This was a request by explorer George William Evans, in a letter to Governor Macquarie in 1815. It has often been asked just why men are gripped with the compulsive drive to explore. The Australian desert explorer Ernest Giles wrote 'An explorer is an explorer from love and it is nature, not art that makes it so.'

The explorers were a diverse band. Some were highly educated government officials with scientific knowledge or surveying skills, others were fine bushmen with a natural talent for exploration, but the overriding love for the Australian landscape was common to all.

Sturt's Party at the junction of the Murray and Darling rivers, 1830

It was said of Charles Sturt, the overland explorer '. . . he quested because of his love for the interior of the continent and his ambition was to reach its very heart.'

Whatever their reasons, many explorers endured dreadful suffering in regions of impenetrable jungle or merciless desert. Colonel Peter Warburton finding water at last, after a particularly tortuous desert crossing wrote in his journal, 'If we press on we risk losing our camels and dying of thirst. If we stand still we starve . . .'

Robert O'Hara Burke and William Wills were stranded with no food at Cooper's Creek, after their incredible trek from the Gulf of Carpentaria. Exhausted and starving they gave up hope and waited for death. Burke's last diary entry read, '. . . weaker than ever . . . my legs and arms are nearly skin and bone.' The only survivor of his party was a man named King. He was found in the care of Aboriginals by Alfred Howitt. His rescuers wrote, '. . . we found King sitting in a hut which the natives had made for him. He seemed exceedingly weak and we found it difficult to follow what he said . . .'

In retrospect, we can see that their judgement was sometimes questionable. For instance in 1770 Captain Cook reported to the British

'Landing of Captain Cook at Botany Bay 1770' by E. Phillips Fox

Admiralty that Botany Bay was '. . . capacious, safe and commodious . . .' While in 1788 Governor Phillip found it to be too exposed and speedily moved the infant colony to Port Jackson, which he considered '. . . the finest in the world, where a thousand sail of the line might ride in the most perfect security.' When the Surveyor General, John Oxley, described land in southern New South Wales as 'uninhabitable and useless for all purposes of civilized man', he would never have dreamed that the 'country south of 34 degrees west of the meridian 147.30 east' would one day become the fertile Murrumbidgee Irrigation Area. Again, Francis Gregory, the leader of the first expedition into the mineral rich Hamersley Range in Western Australia, commented in his journal, '. . . Of minerals I was unable to discover any, except iron.' Sir Thomas Mitchell on the other hand, wrote of the Nandewar Ranges in New South Wales as of 'a beautiful variety of summits', while the Polish explorer, Sir Paul Strzelecki, described Mount Kosciusko, our highest mountain, as 'a craggy, scenic cone cresting the Australian Alps.' It was also with obvious pleasure that Mitchell, exploring the south of the continent, wrote, 'It was not without some pride as a Briton, that I gave the name of the Grampians to these extreme summits of the southern hemisphere.'

The urgency to open up the interior was to enable the colony to expand beyond the confines of the coastal settlements. Although it took place in an atmosphere of excitement and challenge it was mainly for the purpose of gain, a reason for which we may be dubiously proud. However, there is reason to be proud of the intrepid explorers who, with passion and drive, journeyed into the unknown to open up new lands for the eager pioneer settlers.

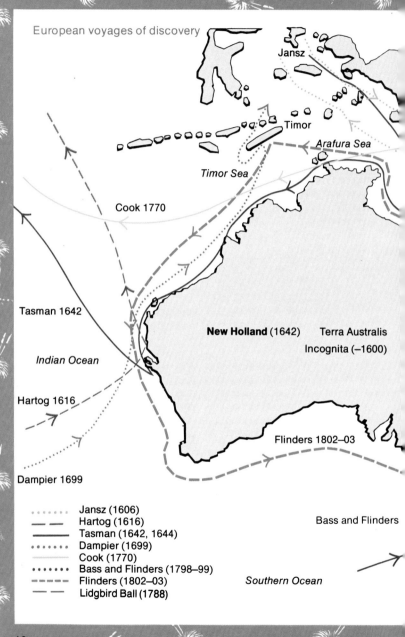

European voyages of discovery

Jansz

Timor

Arafura Sea

Timor Sea

Cook 1770

Tasman 1642

Indian Ocean

Hartog 1616

Dampier 1699

New Holland (1642)   Terra Australis
Incognita (–1600)

Flinders 1802–03

.... Jansz (1606)
‒ ‒ ‒ Hartog (1616)
——— Tasman (1642, 1644)
•••••• Dampier (1699)
——— Cook (1770)
•••••• Bass and Flinders (1798–99)
===== Flinders (1802–03)
‒ ‒ ‒ Lidgbird Ball (1788)

Bass and Flinders

Southern Ocean

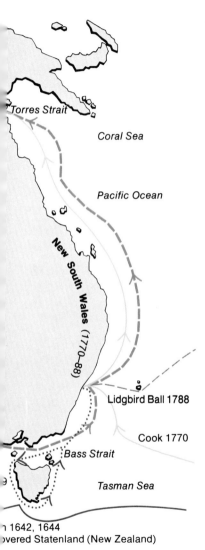

Torres Strait

Coral Sea

Pacific Ocean

New South Wales (1770–88)

Lidgbird Ball 1788

Cook 1770

Bass Strait

Tasman Sea

n 1642, 1644
overed Statenland (New Zealand)

George Bass 1763–1808

A ship's surgeon; together with Matthew Flinders he circumnavigated Van Diemen's Land (Tasmania) in a rowing boat, *Tom Thumb*, in 1798, proving that it was an island.

Gregory Blaxland 1778–1853
William Charles Wentworth 1793–1872
William Lawson 1774–1850

These three men were inland explorers. In 1813 they crossed the Blue Mountains west of Sydney and so opened up the fertile western plains to the colony.

Robert O'Hara Burke 1821–61
William Wills 1834–61

Burke, a policeman, and Wills, a surveyor, were the first Europeans to cross the continent from south to north. In 1860 they trekked from Melbourne to the Gulf of Carpentaria. On their return journey, because of exhaustion and lack of food, they slowly starved to death at Cooper Creek.

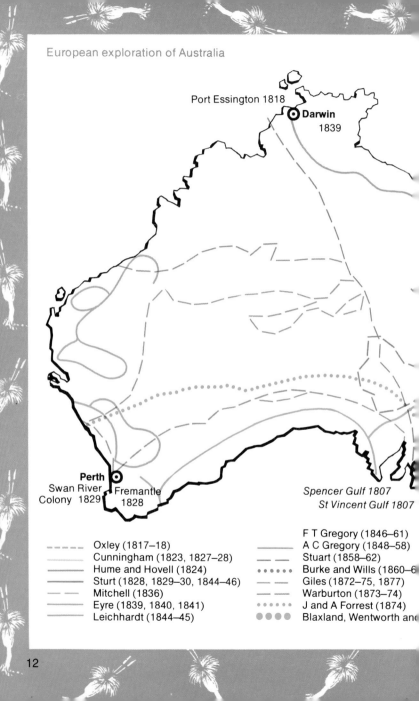

European exploration of Australia

Port Essington 1818

Darwin 1839

Perth
Swan River Colony 1829

Fremantle 1828

Spencer Gulf 1807
St Vincent Gulf 1807

----- Oxley (1817–18)
Cunningham (1823, 1827–28)
Hume and Hovell (1824)
Sturt (1828, 1829–30, 1844–46)
Mitchell (1836)
Eyre (1839, 1840, 1841)
Leichhardt (1844–45)

F T Gregory (1846–61)
A C Gregory (1848–58)
Stuart (1858–62)
•••• Burke and Wills (1860–6
Giles (1872–75, 1877)
Warburton (1873–74)
•••• J and A Forrest (1874)
●●●● Blaxland, Wentworth an

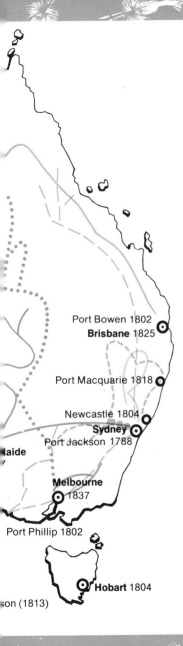

Port Bowen 1802
Brisbane 1825 ⊙

Port Macquarie 1818 ⊙

Newcastle 1804 ⊙
Sydney ⊙
Port Jackson 1788

Adelaide

Melbourne
⊙ 1837

Port Phillip 1802

⊙ **Hobart** 1804

...son (1813)

James Cook 1728–79

Cook landed in Botany Bay in 1770. At Possession Island, Torres Strait, he claimed the eastern coast of Australia in the name of King George III of Great Britain, and named it New South Wales.

William Dampier 1652–1715

A British privateer who visited the western coast of Australia in 1688 and again in 1699.

Edward John Eyre 1815–1901

An inland explorer, he crossed the continent from Streaky Bay, South Australia, to Albany, Western Australia, in 1839–41, a trek of almost 1600 kilometres.

Matthew Flinders 1774–1814

A British naval officer, he circumnavigated Australia in 1801–03, thus allowing the coastal mapping of Australia to be completed.

Dirk Hartog c 1570

A Dutch navigator who landed on an island off Western Australia in 1616, later named after him.

Willem Jansz c 1550

A Dutch sea captain, he gave European navigators the first certain knowledge that Australia existed. In 1606 he landed on the west coast of Cape York Peninsula.

Ludwig Leichhardt 1813–48

He explored inland from Brisbane to Port Essington, Northern Territory, in 1844, a 3200 kilometre trek. In 1848 he and an entire expedition disappeared without a trace, while trying to cross Australia from east to west.

Sir Douglas Mawson 1882–1958

Antarctic explorer and geologist who made many expeditions to the cold continent between 1907 and 1924. He was largely responsible for Australia gaining sovereignty over Antarctica between the 45° and 160° eastern meridians.

John McDouall Stuart 1815–66

He finally crossed the continent from south to north in 1862, after three attempted journeys into the interior.

Charles Sturt 1795–1869

An inland explorer who discovered and named the Murray River in 1829.

Abel Tasman 1602–59

A Dutch navigator, he discovered Van Diemen's Land (Tasmania) and Statenland (New Zealand) in 1642.

Early European discovery and settlement

1642	Van Diemen's Land (Tasmania)	Discovered
1770	Botany Bay	Discovered
1774	Norfolk Island	Discovered
1788	Port Jackson (Sydney)	Settled
1788	Lord Howe Island	Discovered
1802	Spencer Gulf and St Vincent Gulf	Discovered
1802	Port Phillip	Discovered
1804	Newcastle	Settled
1804	Hobart	Settled
1818	Port Macquarie	Settled
1819	Port Essington	Discovered
1825	Brisbane	Settled
1828	Fremantle	Discovered
1829	Swan River Colony (Perth)	Settled
1835	Melbourne	Settled
1836	Adelaide	Settled
1839	Port Darwin	Discovered

Development of a nation

From 1788 to 1850 the government of the colony was in the tight control of New South Wales. Resentment ran high when laws passed by the New South Wales Legislative Assembly, affected newer parts of the colony, hundreds of miles away. In 1850 the Australian Colonies Government Act was forced through Parliament, resulting in responsible government for each of the States. Each State now had its own governor.

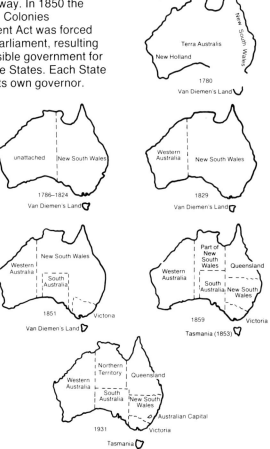

Hollandia Nova

1650
Van Diemen's Land

coastline not completed until 1802

Terra Australis
New Holland
New South Wales

1780
Van Diemen's Land

unattached | New South Wales

1786–1824
Van Diemen's Land

Western Australia | New South Wales

1829
Van Diemen's Land

Western Australia | New South Wales
South Australia

1851
Van Diemen's Land
Victoria

Western Australia | Part of New South Wales | Queensland
South Australia | New South Wales

1859
Tasmania (1853)
Victoria

Western Australia | Northern Territory | Queensland
South Australia | New South Wales
Australian Capital

1931
Tasmania
Victoria

A helping hand with Australian history

'Terra Australis Incognita' was inhabited by its Aboriginal people who had their origins in remote antiquity.

1606 Willem Jansz lands on west coast of Cape York, Queensland.

1616 Dirk Hartog lands on the island later named after him, off the west coast of Australia.

1642 Abel Tasman discovers Van Diemen's Land (Tasmania) and Statenland (New Zealand).

1770 Captain James Cook lands at Botany Bay. He calls the eastern coastline New South Wales in the name of Britain.

1788 Beginning of European settlement as a penal colony. Arrival of Governor Arthur Phillip and First Fleet, at Botany Bay, 18 January, and at Port Jackson on 26 January, when Phillip formally takes possession of the whole of the eastern part of the continent, including Tasmania.

78. *Hobart Town Gazette,* 1843.

1793 First free settlers arrive.

1796 Discovery of coal at Newcastle.

1797 Introduction of merino sheep by John Macarthur.

1798 George Bass and Matthew Flinders circumnavigate Van Diemen's Land (Tasmania).

1802 Discovery of Port Phillip, Victoria, and of Port Bowen, Queensland, by Lieutenant John Murray, and St Vincent Gulf and Spencer Gulf, South Australia, by Matthew Flinders.

DID YOU KNOW?

Ten thousand years ago both the Europeans and the Australian Aboriginals were hunters and gatherers. However, over-population in Europe forced agricultural development, whereas the Aboriginals, with plenty of land, did not have to change their ways.

1804 Lieutenant David Collins establishes settlement at Hobart.

1807 First shipment of saleable wool to England.

1808 The Rum Rebellion. Deposition of Governor William Bligh.

1813 Crossing of Blue Mountains by Gregory Blaxland, William Charles Wentworth and William Lawson.

1814 Matthew Flinders suggests the name Australia instead of New Holland.

1817 Bank of New South Wales, the first bank, is established.

1819 Lt Phillip King discovers Port Essington, Northern Territory.

1822 Establishment of penal settlement at Macquarie Harbour, Tasmania.

1823 Brisbane River discovered by John Oxley and three convicts.

1825 Separation of the administration of Van Diemen's Land from New South Wales. Establishment of settlement of Brisbane.

1828 First census taken: 36 000 convicts and free settlers, 2549 military personnel. No Aboriginals counted.

1829 Foundation of settlement at Swan River, Western Australia. Perth founded.

1834 First settlement at Twofold Bay, New South Wales. Henty brothers form settlement at Portland, Victoria.

1835 Foundation of Melbourne, planned by Governor Sir Richard Bourke.

1836 Settlement founded at Adelaide under Governor Sir John Hindmarsh.

1838 Captain James Bremer establishes Port Essington, Northern Territory.

1839 Port Darwin discovered by crew of the *Beagle*.

1840 Abolition of convict transportation to New South Wales.

1841 New Zealand proclaimed as a separate colony.

1842 First elected council in New South Wales.

Attempted escape

1847 Melbourne proclaimed a city.

1850 Sydney University founded. Representative government granted to Victoria, Tasmania and South Australia.

1851 Edward Hargraves discovers gold at Lewis Ponds, New South Wales. The Port Phillip District is created a separate colony, named Victoria.

1852 Abolition of convict transportation to Van Diemen's Land (Tasmania).

1854 Eureka Stockade riot at Ballarat, Victoria, sparked off by gold-miners' objections to high mining licence fees.

1855 Van Diemen's Land renamed Tasmania, commemorating its discoverer, Abel Tasman. Responsible government granted to New South Wales, Victoria and Tasmania.

1856 Responsible government granted to South Australia.

1857 Granting of the right to vote to adult males in Victoria.

1858 Granting of the right to vote to adult males in New South Wales.

1859 Queensland proclaimed a separate colony.

1863 Northern Territory taken over by South Australia. Discovery of gold at Kalgoorlie, Western Australia.

1864 First sugar made from Queensland cane.

1869 'Welcome Stranger' gold nugget found at Dunolly, Victoria.

1872 Trans-continental telegraph completed. First cable message from Sydney to London.

1876 Death of Truganini, last full-blooded Tasmanian Aboriginal.

1878 First telephone in Australia.

1880 Ned Kelly, bushranger and rebel, captured.

1883 Silver discovered at Broken Hill, New South Wales.

1885 New South Wales contingent sent to Sudan, Africa. Broken Hill Proprietary Silver Mining Company (BHP) floated.

1889 Sir Henry Parkes's 'Tenterfield Address' on federation.

1899 First Australian

DID YOU KNOW?
The secret ballot box, the most prized symbol of democracy, was pioneered in Victoria in 1856.

contingent sent to South Africa to fight with the British in the Boer War.

1900 Federation: on 17 September Australia announced its intention to become independent from Great Britain.

1901 1 January — the first day of the new century — the Commonwealth of Australia was proclaimed. First federal election.
According to the census of 1901, the white population was 3 773 801. Aboriginals were not counted.

1902 Granting of the right to vote in federal elections to women.

1908 Canberra chosen as the site for the federal capital.

1910 First Commonwealth bank notes issued.

1911 Mawson leads expedition to the Antarctic.

1913 First Commonwealth postage stamps issued.

1914 First World War declared; 20 000 troops embark for Europe. German raider, *Emden*, destroyed by HMAS *Sydney* in Indian Ocean. ANZAC (Australian and New Zealand Army Corps) formed.

1915 BHP opens at Newcastle. ANZAC troops land at Gallipoli on 25 April, evacuated on 18 December.

1917 Completion of trans-continental railway. First wireless message from London to Sydney.

1918 Armistice with Germany, 11 November. Australia House, London, opened by King George V.

1919 Return of Australian troops from Europe. Ross and Keith Smith make the first flight from England to Australia. Influenza epidemic sweeps Australia.

1920 Queensland and Northern Territory Aerial Services (QANTAS) formed by Hudson Fysh. White population 5 411 300.

1922 Queensland is the first state to abolish the death penalty.

1923 Sydney Harbour Bridge commenced.

1926 Auction sales of wool begun.

1927 Seat of government moved from Melbourne to Canberra.

1928 Kingsford Smith flies from America to Australia in *Southern Cross*. Flying Doctor service begun. First traffic lights in Australia installed in Melbourne.

1929 Beginning of Depression. Fall in exports. Commonwealth government mobilises gold reserves.

1932 Sydney Harbour Bridge opened. Lang government in New South Wales dismissed.

1933 BHP takes over steel works at Port Kembla, New South Wales.

1935 Kingsford Smith lost without trace near the Bay of Bengal, flying from England to Australia. Ansett Airways set up by Reginald Ansett.

1936 Hume reservoir completed.

1938 Coca Cola is first made in Australia.

1939 Second World War declared. The last grain clipper race to England held.

1940 20 000 Australian troops embark for service abroad. Introduction of food and fuel rationing.

1941 Sinking of HMAS *Sydney* and HMAS *Canberra*. Australian troops besieged at Tobruk.

1942 Darwin bombed. Fall of Singapore. Battle of the Coral Sea. Japanese midget submarines in Sydney Harbour.

1943 Industrial conscription introduced.

1944 Pay-as-you-earn taxation begun. Japanese prisoners of war attempt mass breakout at Cowra, New South Wales; 234 killed.

1945 Second World War ends; demobilisation of 500 000 men and women begun.

1946 United Nations grants trusteeship of New Guinea to Australia.

1947 Commonwealth Arbitration Commission established. Arthur Calwell's immigration drive begun.

1948 Forty-hour week established. First Holden car made by General Motors-Holden. Meat and clothes rationing ends.

1949 The right to vote granted to certain Aboriginals. Snowy Mountains Hydro-Electric Scheme commenced. An attempt to nationalise banks defeated. Prime Minister Ben Chifley deposed. Liberals come to power under Robert Menzies.

1950 Petrol rationing ends. Australian troops join United Nations force in Korea.

1951 Melbourne becomes an international airport.

1952 ANZUS Security Treaty signed in Washington.

Discovery of uranium at Rum Jungle, Northern Territory. Nuclear experiments begun at Australian National University.

1953 Atomic Energy Commission established. Television Bill passed. Atomic weapons tested by United Kingdom at Woomera, South Australia. Wool prices drop after four year boom. South East Asia Treaty Organisation (SEATO) founded.

1954 Queen Elizabeth II makes the first visit to Australia by a reigning monarch. Uranium discovered at Mary Kathleen, Queensland. Troops withdrawn from Korea.
'Petrov Affair' — accusations of Communist espionage in Department of External Affairs. Petrov defects.

1955 Opposition Labor Party splits.
Severe floods in eastern Australia cause havoc.

1956 Olympic Games in Melbourne.

1958 The first nuclear reactor opened at Lucas Heights, Sydney.

1960 Aboriginals become Australian citizens and so become eligible for social service benefits.

Reserve Bank established.

1961 Huge iron-ore deposits found at Pilbara, Western Australia.

1962 Standard-gauge railway track opened between Brisbane, Sydney and Melbourne. Aboriginals granted the vote. Australia grants approval to the United States to build communication base at Exmouth, Western Australia, and space tracking station at Tidbinbilla, near Canberra.

1964 HMAS *Voyager* sinks after collision with HMAS *Melbourne*; 82 lives lost. First flight of Blue Streak rocket launched at Woomera, South Australia.

1965 Australian infantry battalion sent to Vietnam. Australia imposes economic sanctions against the Smith regime in Rhodesia.

1966 On 14 February decimal currency introduced. Aboriginals appeal to the United Nations for human rights. Prime Minister Sir Robert Menzies retires. Gough Whitlam becomes leader of the Labor Party. The phasing in of the metric system of weights and measures begun.

1967 Prime Minister Harold Holt disappears at Portsea, Victoria. John McEwen acts as prime minister. Aboriginals included in census figures for the first time. Demonstration in Melbourne against the hanging of Ronald Ryan, the last person to be hanged in Australia.

1968 First Australian heart transplant performed. John Gorton becomes leader of the Liberal Party and prime minister.

1969 HMAS *Melbourne* collides with USS *Frank E Evans* with the loss of 74 lives. Indian–Pacific railway completed. Poseidon company announces a find of nickel; as a result, share prices soar. Robert Hawke is elected president of the Australian Council of Trade Unions (ACTU). Arbitration Commission grants equal pay to women for work of equal value.

1970 Vietnam Moratoriums: large-scale demonstrations against Australian and United States involvement in Vietnam war. Mineral

shares boom ends. Tullamarine airport opened in Melbourne.

1971 Liberal–Country Party coalition in government under leadership of Prime Minister William McMahon. Australia ends fighting role in Vietnam. Lake Pedder in Tasmania is flooded as part of a hydro-electric scheme.

1972 Australian Labor Party wins victory under the leadership of Gough Whitlam. Withdrawal of troops from Vietnam. Formal ending of White Australia Policy.

1973 Eighteen-year-olds are granted the right to vote in federal elections. Queen Elizabeth II to be known as Queen of Australia.

1974 Cyclone Tracy hits Darwin, Northern Territory (Christmas Day). Bankcard is introduced. Fully elected assemblies set up in the Northern Territory and Australian Capital Territory.

1975 Dismissal of Whitlam government by Governor-General Sir John Kerr. Return of Liberal–Country Party coalition to power under leadership of Malcolm Fraser. Papua

New Guinea becomes independent. No-fault divorce introduced. The MV *Lake Illawarra* collides with the Tasman Bridge, Hobart. Five Australian journalists are killed in East Timor.

1976 Flexitime is approved for federal public servants.

1977 Granville train disaster; 81 die.

1978 Northern Territory becomes responsible for its own administration.

1979 Aboriginal Land Trust by now gains title to 144 properties, all formerly Aboriginal reserves.

1980 Campbell Inquiry into Australian financial system. Nugan Hand Bank collapses. The disappearance of baby Azaria Chamberlain at Ayers Rock.

1981 Severe drought affects large areas of Australia. Andrew Peacock resigns as Foreign Affairs Minister.

1982 New South Wales introduces random breath testing of drivers. The Franklin Dam controversy rages in Tasmania. Lindy Chamberlain found guilty of the murder of her daughter, Azaria.

1983 Prime Minister Malcolm Fraser requests and is granted a double dissolution of parliament and an election of both houses follows. The Labor Party sweeps into office under the leadership of Robert Hawke. Ash Wednesday (devastating bushfires in South Australia and Victoria). America's Cup victory by *Australia II*.

1984 Government, business and union leaders reach accord on prices and income policy. Control of Ayers Rock given to a group of Aboriginals. December federal elections return Labor Party to government under the leadership of Prime Minister Robert Hawke.

1985 McClelland Royal Commission into British nuclear tests in Australia. Justice Lionel Murphy of the High Court of Australia is acquitted on one charge but scheduled for re-trial for another charge of allegedly having conspired to pervert the course of justice. The Federal Treasury allows the application for a banking licence by 16 foreign banks.

1986 Queen Elizabeth II, on her visit to Canberra, signs a proclamation which finally severs some of Australia's historical, political and legal ties with the United Kingdom. By the virtue of such a proclamation the Australia Act of 1986 comes into force. Lindy Chamberlain is released on licence from Berrimah gaol, Darwin. Bombing of Russell Street Police Headquarters in Melbournes shocks Australia. Perfect conditions for viewing Halley's Comet in the area around Siding Springs, New South Wales, creates world wide interest. Two Australians, Kevin Barlow and Brian Chambers, are convicted of drug trafficking and subsequently hung in Malaysia. A fringe benefits tax is introduced. In a landmark decision, the High Court rules against the Australasian Meatworker's Union in a dispute over wages and conditions between this union and the Mudginberri Station (abattoirs) in Western Australia. Pope Paul II travels more than 10 000 kilometres on his extensive tour of Australia. The Turkish consulate in Melbourne is destroyed by terrorists. Justice Lionel Murphy of the High Court dies.

1987

The working commission of inquiry into the Chamberlain's conviction results in the charges against Lindy and Michael Chamberlain being quashed.
Four men found guilty and one pleaded guilty of murder in the Anita Cobby Trial.
The Milperra massacre trial — the longest running in NSW legal history ended with 7 men being found guilty of murder, 21 guilty of manslaughter and 31 guilty of affray.
The July federal elections result in the re-election of the Labor Party to power under the leadership of Prime Minister Robert Hawke.
The Australian share market collapses.
Sir Joh Bjelke-Petersen resigns as Premier of Queensland.

The way we were

Dread, doubt, despair, brutality, horror, sadism, the lash, injustice, famine, hangings, murder, revolt, floggings, disease, pestilence, depravity, thieving . . . a worthy scenario for a modern horror movie? In actual fact it is a list of words often used to describe our history since 1788. From the very first, when Governor Phillip desperately sought better supplies and conditions for the 'wretched felons' from the overcrowded British prisons, who were about to make the hazardous journey to New South Wales, the story was one of desperation and brutality.

The struggling infant colony began with bitter disappointment. Lack of food, constant sickness, and indolence seemed to set the pattern for the years to come. The country appeared to be a huge and empty land, hostile to British ideas and ways. The colony also had conflicting obligations. It had to contend with the commercial demands of the British Government as well as with the needs of a new penal colony. There were no encouraging signs for anyone to feel that the foundation of a prosperous nation could be made from such a hopeless beginning.

Gradually, the tenacity of the colonists and their improved understanding of the land, led to better times. At the same time, explorers blazed tracks into the interior and people began to spill out of the overcrowded towns and cities and into the country. Terms such as pioneers, squatters, emancipists, chain gangs, currency lads, new chums, cattle duffers, honest battlers, bolters, free selectors and bushrangers all became part of Australian phraseology, and a spirit of self-reliance seemed to flourish in isolated communities. Compared to the confines of the English countryside there was space to breathe in this far off colony in the antipodes, and the people liked it.

'The days of gold', from the 1850s to 1880s, brought an uninterrupted boom to the colony, and tradesmen, clerks, shepherds and sailors all headed for the gold fields gripped by 'gold fever'. Any kind of order in the towns or cities was disrupted, and although 'great excitement prevailed' and 'whole towns were in hysterics', Lieutenant Governor La Trobe of Victoria contemptuously remarked, 'The whole structure of society and the whole machinery of government is dislocated.' Though trouble intermittently flared up on the gold fields, due to various injustices and persecutions, the only major rebellion of the period and of the whole of Australian history, took place at the Eureka Stockade near Ballarat in December 1854.

Towards the latter part of the 19th century, railways and improved roads brought the country closer to the city and a new feeling of nationalism was born. Constitutionally, there was no such thing as an Australian citizen or an Australian nation, but people from both town and country wanted to be counted as one.

In his Tenterfield Oration of 1889, referring to the joining of all States in a federation, the revered statesman, Sir Henry Parkes said, 'Surely what the Americans have done by war, the Australians could bring about by peace without breaking the ties that hold them to the mother country . . . We ought to set about creating this great national government for all Australia'.

The Commonwealth of Australia was proclaimed on the first day of the new century, 1st January 1901. Sir Edmund Barton — the first prime minister of Australia remarked, 'For the first time in history we have a continent for a nation and a nation for a continent.'

Horse-drawn carriage 1870s

Arrival of first railway train, Parramatta from Sydney

Sydney Cove, Port Jackson 1788

A nation coming of age (1900–1988)

Although the young Commonwealth began the new century on a note of cautious optimism it was obvious that it needed to be awakened to the demands of such a monumental experiment as federation.

To establish a new identity was the main concern of most Australians, but the old loyalties and demands of Britain were strong. Australian 'soldiers of the Queen' marched off to fight the Boer War in South Africa, one which many saw as '. . . the most iniquitous war ever waged.'

Nevertheless, times were rapidly changing. The Commonwealth had blundered into a new century and progress came at a bewildering pace. In 1905 the Pure Foods Act ensured quality and purity of food substantially reducing infant mortality. Electricity had replaced gas lights, trams, trains and cars had superseded the horse and the new inventions of wireless, cash registers and typewriters all led to an increasing demand in skill. This was the machine age and opportunity was everywhere demanding that everyone become literate. The workers backed trade unions and a five and a half day week and a £2/2/0 or $4.20 average weekly wage was introduced. Change was in the air worldwide and Australia was making great strides in coming of age and keeping up with the rest of the world.

Yet loyalty to Britain persisted. When war broke out in 1914, Australians again fought thousands of miles away from home. On 25 April 1915, the A.N.Z.A.C.s began the bitter campaign against the Turks in Gallipoli and a shocked nation learned of the long casualty list. All told 416 809 men volunteered for the war, of which 59 258 were killed or reported missing in action.

Times were confusing for the returning 'digger'. They were years of uncertain prosperity, followed by the Great Depression of 1929–32. The disaster affected all Australians: at one stage 30% of the workforce was unemployed and those lucky enough to keep a job had restricted working hours or cut wages.

Although suspicions of Japan's intentions in 1939 were mounting, it was the troubles in Europe again which plunged Australia into the Second World War. By 1945, 993 000 persons had enlisted. As the casualty list grew, news from such places as the Middle East, Greece, North

Africa, Tobruk was eagerly sought. On 8 December 1941, the Prime Minister, Mr Curtin, announced that Australia was at war with Japan. Singapore, Borneo, Java, New Guinea, Kokoda Trail, Coral Sea, Rabaul, Owen Stanley Range and Changi prison became hushed household words. In 1942 Darwin was bombed with a loss of 238 lives. The war in Europe ended in May 1945, and under the threat of a widening of atomic warfare, after the bombing of Hiroshima and Nagasaki, the Japanese surrendered on 14 August 1945.

The post war years brought growth and prosperity. With the signing of the ANZUS pact, Australia was at last making decisions without reference to Britain. In the 'cold war' atmosphere of the 50s, Australian troops joined the British Commonwealth Brigade in Korea. Increased production and labour shortages brought full employment and the rural and home building industries flourished. A forty hour week was introduced and the basic wage was £5/16/- or $11.60. A new immigration drive resulted in a more tolerant attitude towards Europeans and their cultures and public awareness of the plight of the Australian Aboriginal evolved. Education became more readily available and there was more time for leisure and cultural pursuits.

During the 60s there was a time of affluence and prosperity with the mineral's boom. Few people took notice of the war in Asia. However, the government argued that to retain the United States' protection through the newly formed SEATO alliance, Australia must support the United States in Vietnam. Over 50 000 troops served in the war with 400 deaths and 2000 injured. A moratorium clearly demonstrated that the majority of Australians were against our involvement and after world wide pressure, the U.S.A. ceased hostilities.

General dissatisfaction in the 70s and 80s saw political parties come and go with a new wave of unrest sweeping the country. The White Australia Policy was dropped and Asian migration was encouraged. Automation dramatically changed technology and workers displaced by computers joined the long list of unemployed.

The grand experiment, begun in 1900 with federation, has brought great triumphs and many difficulties, but over the past eighty years Australia has come of age and has managed to take its place in the world scene with dignity and assurance.

Population

The Australian population in 1987 is estimated to be around 16 000 000. Of the population 88 per cent are urban dwellers and settlement is mostly on the fertile coastal plains. The average population density is two persons per square kilometre. A striking feature of Australia's population is the large number of immigrants who have settled here since the Second World War. At present, one in every four persons is either a first or second generation settler.

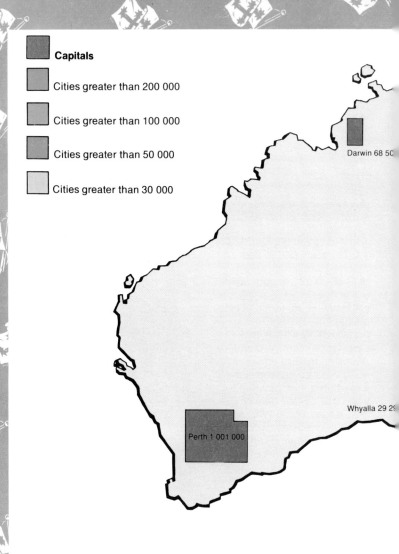

Capitals

Cities greater than 200 000

Cities greater than 100 000

Cities greater than 50 000

Cities greater than 30 000

Darwin 68 5[0]

Whyalla 29 2[9]

Perth 1 001 000

DID YOU KNOW?

A 1985 survey recorded 5 093 920 households in
Australia (nearly 3.1 persons to each household.)

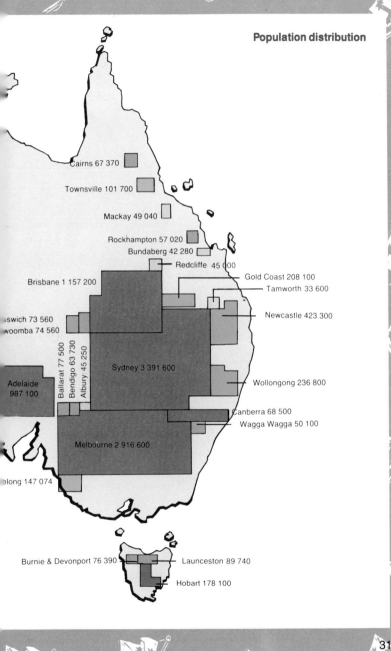

Population distribution

Cairns 67 370

Townsville 101 700

Mackay 49 040

Rockhampton 57 020

Bundaberg 42 280

Redcliffe 45 000

Brisbane 1 157 200

Gold Coast 208 100

Tamworth 33 600

Ipswich 73 560

Toowoomba 74 560

Newcastle 423 300

Ballarat 77 500

Bendigo 63 730

Albury 45 250

Sydney 3 391 600

Adelaide 987 100

Wollongong 236 800

Canberra 68 500

Wagga Wagga 50 100

Melbourne 2 916 600

Geelong 147 074

Burnie & Devonport 76 390

Launceston 89 740

Hobart 178 100

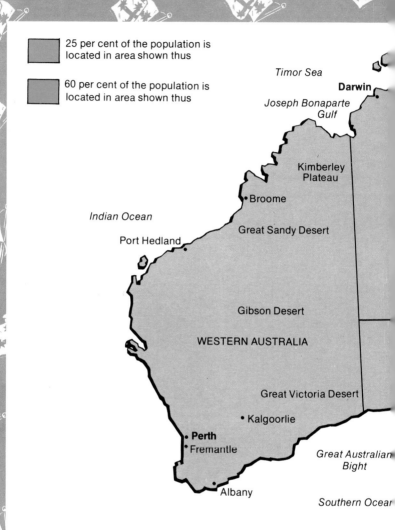

Map legend

25 per cent of the population is located in area shown thus

60 per cent of the population is located in area shown thus

Timor Sea

Darwin

Joseph Bonaparte Gulf

Kimberley Plateau

• Broome

Indian Ocean

Great Sandy Desert

Port Hedland •

Gibson Desert

WESTERN AUSTRALIA

Great Victoria Desert

• Kalgoorlie

• **Perth**
• Fremantle

Great Australian Bight

• Albany

Southern Ocean

DID YOU KNOW?

Marital figures for Australia (1985) show 7.3 marriages per 1000 people. Median age for brides is 23.2 years. Median age for bridegrooms is 25.4 years.

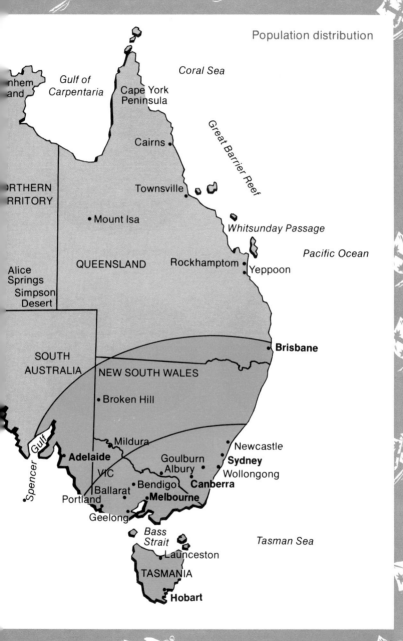

Population distribution

Population changes since federation

▲ % of people living in Australia, but born elsewhere
▲ % of native born Australians

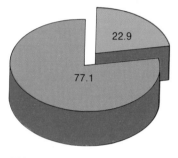

22.9

77.1

1900 total population 3 765 300

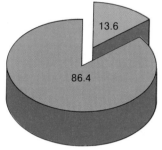

13.6

86.4

1930 total population 6 500 800

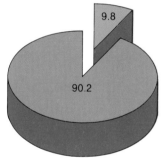

9.8

90.2

1947 total population 7 579 400

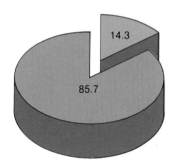

14.3

85.7

1955 total population 9 311 800

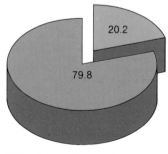

20.2

79.8

1971 total population 13 067 300

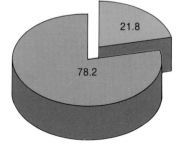

21.8

78.2

1981 total population 14 923 300

Total population (15 973 900) as of June, 1986.

Overseas-born 21.3%

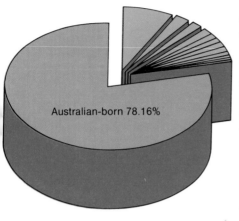

British Isles	7.5%
Germany	.77%
Greece	0.96%
Italy	1.7%
Yugoslavia	0.99%
Other European countries	2.9%
China	0.2%
Other Asian Countries	3.3%
Africa	0.72%
Americas	0.76%
Pacific island	1.5%
TOTAL	21.3%

Australian-born 78.16%

Birthplace of overseas born

British Isles

England, Wales, Scotland, Northern Ireland; the Republic of Ireland.

Europe

Albania, Austria, Belgium, Bulgaria, Czechoslovakia, Denmark, Estonia, Finland, France, Germany, Greece, Hungary, Italy, Latvia, Lithuania, Malta, Netherlands, Norway, Poland, Portugal, Romania, Spain, Sweden, Switzerland, Ukraine, USSR, Yugoslavia.

Middle East

Israel, Lebanon, Syria, Turkey, Egypt.

Asia

Burma, China, Hong Kong, India, Indonesia, Japan, Malaysia, Pakistan, Philippines, Singapore, Sri Lanka, Vietnam.

Africa

Mauritius, South Africa.

Americas

United States, Canada, South America, West Indies Federation.

Pacific Islands

Fiji, New Caledonia, Vanuatu, New Zealand.

Immigration to Australia

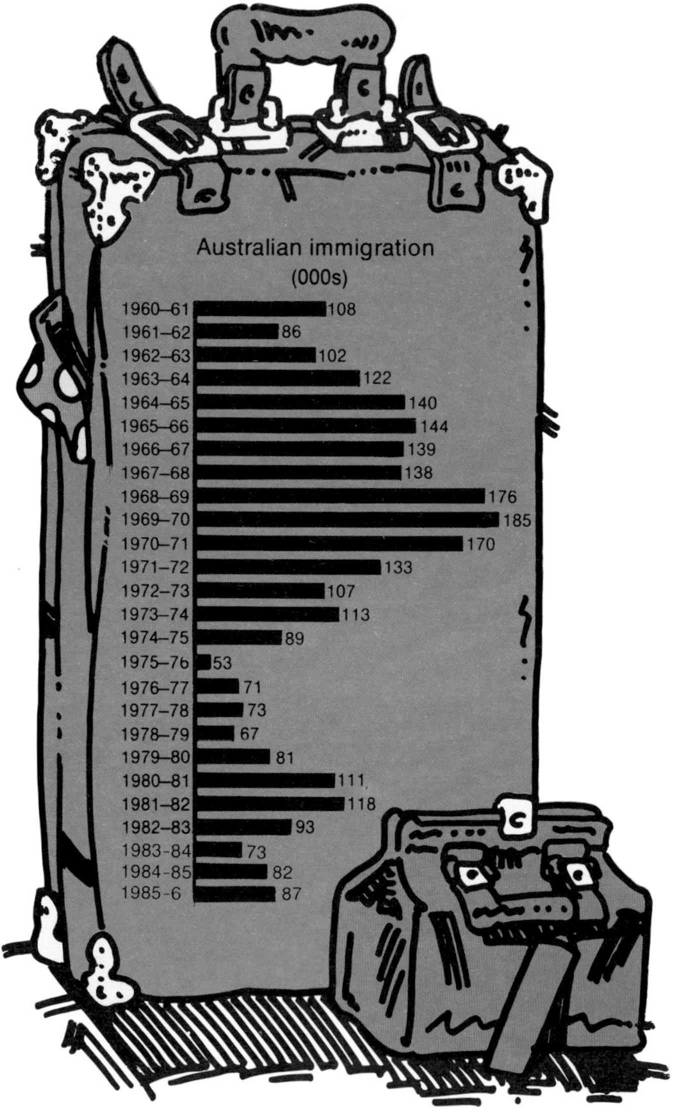

Australian immigration
(000s)

Year	Immigration (000s)
1960–61	108
1961–62	86
1962–63	102
1963–64	122
1964–65	140
1965–66	144
1966–67	139
1967–68	138
1968–69	176
1969–70	185
1970–71	170
1971–72	133
1972–73	107
1973–74	113
1974–75	89
1975–76	53
1976–77	71
1977–78	73
1978–79	67
1979–80	81
1980–81	111
1981–82	118
1982–83	93
1983–84	73
1984–85	82
1985-6	87

Comparison of Aboriginal and European populations

Aboriginal population	European population	
(census estimates only before 1967)		
1788	300 000	1 030
1860	22 200	1 145 600
1900	93 300	3 765 300
1910	80 100	4 425 100
1920	71 800	5 411 300
1930	80 700	6 500 800
1947	76 000	7 579 400
1960	84 500	10 391 900

In 1967 the Australian Constitution was changed to stop the specific exclusion of Aboriginals from the census. In 1971 Aboriginals were included in the census for the first time.   Total

			Total
1971	106 300	12 961 000	13 067 300
1981	144 600	14 778 700	14 923 300
1985	estimated total population		15 751 500
1986	estimated total population		15 909 400
1987	projected total for June		16 000 000

Aboriginal population

Because of the difficulty of obtaining accurate counts, until 1930 only estimates were made. An estimate of the number of Aboriginals in Australia at the time of European settlement was thought to be 300 000, but current research suggests that the figure could have been as high as 500 000.

With European settlement, the Aboriginal population declined drastically due to the introduction of disease (to which the Aboriginal had no natural immunity), alcohol and violent conflict.

By the early 1930s the Aboriginal population had decreased to just over 80 000. With increased expenditure on welfare and health, the population decline had reversed by the 1950s.

DID YOU KNOW?

The oldest skeleton found in Australia was at Lake Mungo in south-west New South Wales. It is believed to be 38 000 years old and is the skeleton of a female. It has traces of ceremonial ochre (a sign of culture), which is thought to be the oldest sign of use of ochre ever discovered.

The national flag

The red ensign

Flags

For many years the Australian Blue Ensign was regarded as the official flag. This was a plain blue flag, with the Union Jack in the upper corner of the hoist, together with the seven-pointed Commonwealth star beneath. It also contained the five-starred Southern Cross. However it had not been clearly established that any particular flag was the national flag. In 1951 King George VI approved a recommendation by the government that the Australian Blue Ensign be proclaimed the national flag, and the Australian Red Ensign be the proper colour for merchant ships registered in Australia. The *Flags Act* was passed in 1953 by the Commonwealth parliament, making these the official flags of the Commonwealth.

The state flags are based on the plain Blue Ensign with the particular badge of each state added. The Northern Territory flag is based on colours found in desert regions, and the Territory's badge is added.

Coat of arms

The present coat of arms was granted in 1912 by King George V, following approval of substantial alterations by

The national coat of arms

the Commonwealth govern-
ment. It consists of a shield
composed of six parts, each
containing one of the state
badges. These are surrounded by an ermine border,
signifying the federation of
the states into the
Commonwealth. The shield is
supported by two Australian
animals, the kangaroo and
the emu, standing on
ornamental rests, behind
which are small branches of
wattle. The crest consists of
the seven-pointed
Commonwealth gold star, a
symbol of national unity. At
the base of the shield is a
scroll on which is printed the
word 'Australia'.

Anthems

The royal anthem, 'God Save
the Queen', is used in the
presence of Her Majesty the
Queen or a member of the
royal family.

The vice-regal salute, which
consists of the first four and
last four bars of the tune
'Advance Australia Fair', is
used in the presence of the
governor-general.

The national anthem,
'Advance Australia Fair', is
used on all other ceremonial
occasions. For the words of
Australia's national anthem,
see p 161.

Colours

Green and gold are the
national colours of Australia,
and are used on all
appropriate occasions such
as the Olympic Games.

*Unofficial national floral
emblem: wattle*

National animal emblem: kangaroo

DID YOU KNOW?
Ayers Rock is almost at the centre of the Australian
continent. As the crow flies it is 2100 kilometres from
Sydney, 1450 kilometres from Darwin, 1300 kilometres
from Adelaide and 1600 kilometres from Perth.

Public holidays and special days

January	1	New Year's Day
	26	Australia Day (public holiday on Monday following)

March

First Monday	Western Australia: Labour Day
	Tasmania: Eight-Hour Day
Second Monday	Victoria: Labour Day and Moomba Parade
Third Monday	Australian Capital Territory: Labour Day

April

First full moon after equinox (may fall in March)	Easter holiday begins on Good Friday and continues until following Monday (in some states Easter Tuesday is also a public holiday)
25	Anzac Day

May

First Monday	Queensland: Labour Day
	Northern Territory: May Day Holiday

June

Second Monday	Queen's Birthday (except Western Australia)

August

1	Wattle Day (some states)
First Monday	New South Wales: Bank Holiday

September 1 Wattle Day (some states)

October

First Monday	New South Wales and Australian Capital Territory: Labour Day
6	Western Australia: Queen's Birthday
Second Monday	South Australia: Labour Day

November

First Tuesday	Victoria: Melbourne Cup Day
11	Remembrance Day

December	25	Christmas Day
	26	Boxing Day (except South Australia)
	28	South Australia: Proclamation Day

Place

Geography

Location

Australia is a continental land mass lying on, and extending south from, the Tropic of Capricorn in the southern hemisphere. It lies between the Indian and Pacific oceans, with Timor 640 kilometres to the north west, New Guinea 200 kilometres to the north, and New Zealand 1920 kilometres to the south-east and Antarctica 2000 kilometres due south.

Area

The area of Australia is 7 682 300 square kilometres. Australia is about the size of the mainland states of the United States, excluding Alaska, and approximately twenty-four times the size of the British Isles.

Distances

Mainland east–west, 3983 kilometres; north–south, 3138 kilometres. Coastline, including Tasmania and off-shore islands, 36 735 kilometres.

41

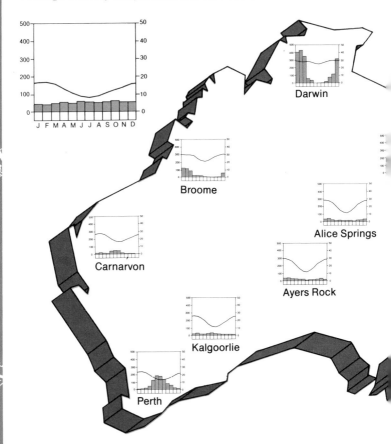

Darwin

Broome

Carnarvon

Alice Springs

Ayers Rock

Kalgoorlie

Perth

Blocks show rainfall in millimetres
Curves show temperature in degrees Celsius

DID YOU KNOW?
The highest recorded temperature of 53.1°C was at
Cloncurry. Queensland, on 16 January 1889.

42

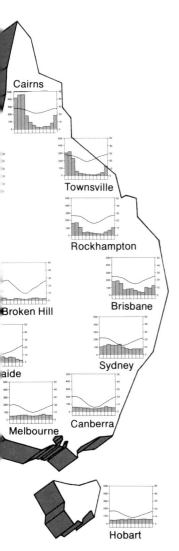

Landform

Australia is the smallest, flattest continent and mostly consists of one vast ancient crustal block, the western plateau, 300 metres above sea level. Another large portion is the central eastern lowlands, which formed the beds of ancient seas. Lowest elevation, Lake Eyre, is 16 metres below sea level. The third area is the eastern highlands, running north and south along the eastern coastline. This is the Great Dividing Range, with Mt Kosciusko its highest peak, 2228 metres above sea level.

Climate

Although varied because of the size of the continent, Australia's climate has no great extremes. Above the Tropic of Capricorn the temperature is generally 23–26°C. In the arid plateaus and deserts of the interior there are hot days and cold nights. The southern states are temperate. Irregular floods and droughts are experienced. Australia is the driest continent on earth.

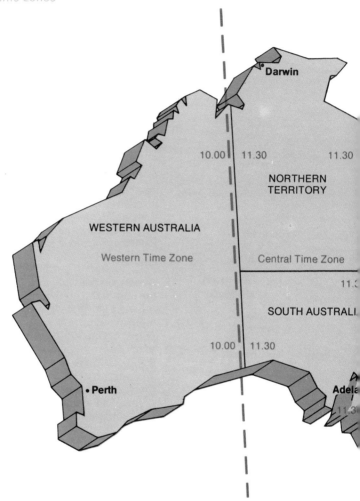

Darwin

10.00 | 11.30   11.30

NORTHERN
TERRITORY

WESTERN AUSTRALIA

Western Time Zone   Central Time Zone

11.3

SOUTH AUSTRALI

10.00 | 11.30

• Perth   Adela

11.3

DID YOU KNOW?
The expected life-span for the average Australian male is
72.32 years and for the Australian female 78.76 years.

2.00

QUEENSLAND

Eastern Time Zone

12.00

Brisbane.

NEW SOUTH WALES

(11.30)
.**Broken Hill**   12.00

12.00

Sydney .

VICTORIA

.**Melbourne**

.**Hobart**

TASMANIA

Time zones

New South Wales, Victoria, South Australia and Tasmania, follow Eastern Summer Time. This is subject to change, but it usually falls in the months of November, December, January and February, and can extend for two weeks longer either side.

Standard time zones

| 0° | 30° | 60° | 90° | 120° | 150° |

gain

Great Britain

Germany

France

Greece

Spain

Italy

Turkey

Gibraltar

Algeria

Iraq

Afghanistan

Iran

Pakistan

Libya

Egypt

Saudi Arabia

Bangladesh

Ethiopia

India

Sri Lanka

Malaysia

Hong Kong

Philippines

Borneo

Uganda

Singapore

Papua N

Nicobar Is

Indonesia

Zimbabwe

Cocos Is

South Africa

Mauritius

Christmas Island

Australia

Nor

Cape of Good Hope

Indian Ocean

McDonald Islands
Heard Island

Union of Soviet Socialist Republics

Manchuria

China

Japan

Universal Time Constant

noon

| −10 | −9 | −8 | −7 | −6 | −5 | −4 | −3 | −2 | −1 | 0 | + |
| 2 am | 3 am | 4 am | 5 am | 6 am | 7 am | 8 am | 9 am | 10 am | 11 am | 12 | 1 |

hours later than Universal Time Constant

DID YOU KNOW?

The world's largest cattle station, 30 028.3 square kilometres, is Strangeray Springs in South Australia. It is almost the same size as Belgium.

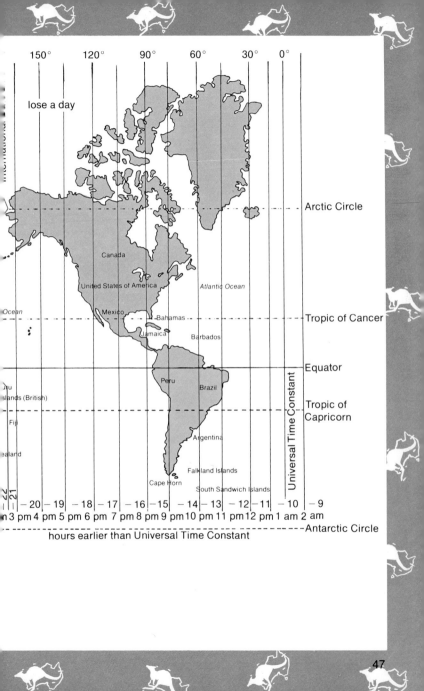

United Kingdom

Gibraltar · Malta · Cyprus

Gambia
Sierra Leone · Nigeria
Ghana
Uganda · Kenya
Tanzania
Zambia
Malawi
Zimbabwe
Botswana · Swaziland
Lesotho

Bangladesh
India
Hong Kong
Sri Lanka
Lakshadweep · Malaysia · Brunei
Seychelles · Singapore · Papua New Guinea
Nicobar Is
Cocos Is
Mauritius · Christmas Island · Australia

Gilbert Islands
· Nauru
· Tuvalu
Kiribati
· Solomon Islands

Norfolk Island
· Western Samoa
Fiji · Cook Island
Tonga

Lord Howe Is
New Zealand

McDonald Islands
Heard Island

Campbell Island

 Commonwealth nations

DID YOU KNOW?
Of all coloured peoples, the Australian Aboriginals are
ethnologically most akin to Caucasians.

Australia in the Commonwealth

The Commonwealth of Nations is a world-wide association of nations and their dependent territories, which recognises the British monarch as its titular head.

The members share many customs and traditions because of their association with the former British Empire, of which all formed a part. These include parliamentary systems of government, judicial systems and educational institutions which are similar to those of the United Kingdom. Although English is the official language, it is used widely in only eight member countries.

The main function of the Commonwealth is to encourage communication, exchange ideas, and develop mutual aid between its member nations.

Canada

Bermuda
Bahamas
Jamaica
Belize
St Vincent
Barbados
Grenada Dominica
Trinidad and Tobago
Guyana

· St Helena

Falkland Islands

· South Sandwich Islands
South Shetland Islands
· South Orkney Islands

Members of the Commonwealth of Nations and their dependencies

Member nations with dependencies	Status of dependency	Member nations with dependencies	Status of dependency
Australia		Nigeria	
Australian Antarctic	Territory	Papua New Guinea	
Christmas Is	Territory	St Lucia , St Vincent & the Grenadiers	Associated st
Cocos Is	Territory	Seychelles	
Coral Sea Is	Territory	Sierra Leone	
Heard & McDonald Is	Territory	Singapore	
Lord Howe Is	Territory	Solomon Is	
Macquarie Is	Territory	Sri Lanka	
Norfolk Is	Territory	Swaziland	
Bahamas		Tanzania	
Bangladesh		Tonga	
Barbados		Trinidad & Tobago	
Belize		Tuvalu	
Botswana		United Kingdom	
Brunei		Anguilla	Colc
Canada		Antigua	Associated st
Cook Is		Barbuda	
Cyprus		Bermuda	Colc
Dominica		British Antarctic	
Fiji		British Indian Ocean	
Gambia		British Virgin Is	Colc
Ghana		Cayman Is	Colo
Grenada		Dominica	Associated sta
Guyana		Falkland Is	Colc
India		Gibraltar	Colc
Jamaica		Hong Kong	
Kenya		Montserrat	Colc
Kiribati		Pitcairn	Colc
Lesotho		St Helena	Colc
Malawi		St Christopher-Nevis	
Malaysia		St Kitts–Nevis	Associated sta
Maldives		Turks & Caicos Is	Associated sta
Malta		Uganda	
Mauritius		Vanuatu	
Nauru		Western Samoa	
New Zealand	Territory & associated states	Zambia	
Niue & Tokelau Is		Zimbabwe	

USSR

Asia

Mongolia

North Korea

Sea of Japan

Japan

hanistan

China

South Korea

Nepal

Bangladesh

ropic of Cancer

Laos

kistan

Vietnam

Taiwan

Hong Kong

India

Burma

South China Sea

Philippines

Cambodia

Malaysia

Borneo

West Irian

Papua New Guinea

Equator

Sumatra

Melanesia

Arafura Sea

Solomon Islands

Java

Timor

Vanuatu

Christmas Island (Australia)

Sulawesi

Cocos Islands (Australia)

Coral Sea

Tropic of Capricorn

New Caledonia

Australia

Indian Ocean

Norfolk Island (Australia)

Lord Howe Island (Australia)

Kangaroo Island (Australia)

New Zealand

Heard and McDonald Islands

Tasmania

Tasman Sea

Pacific Ocean

Macquarie Island (Australia)

Casey

Australian Antarctic Territory

Davis

Mawson

DID YOU KNOW?

Australia is the world's largest inhabited island and the smallest continent. It is also the largest continent occupied by one nation and the least populated.

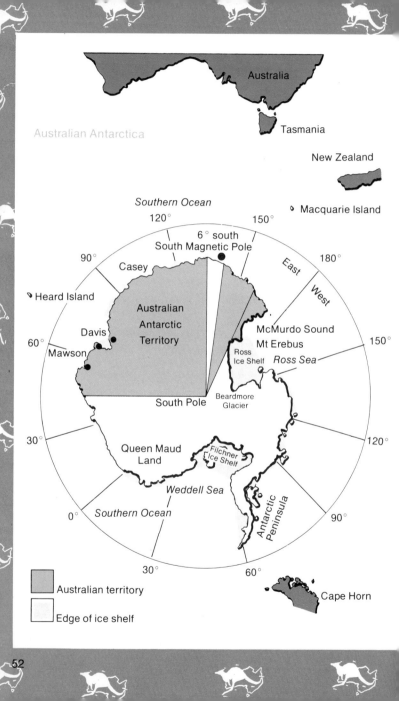

Australia

Tasmania

Australian Antarctica

New Zealand

○ Macquarie Island

Southern Ocean

120°   150°

6° south
South Magnetic Pole ●

90°   180°

Casey   East   West

○ Heard Island

Australian
Antarctic
Territory   McMurdo Sound
Mt Erebus

60°   Davis   *Ross Sea*   150°

Mawson   Ross
Ice Shelf ○

South Pole   Beardmore
Glacier

30°   120°

Queen Maud
Land   Filchner
Ice Shelf

Weddell Sea

0°   *Southern Ocean*   90°

30°   60°   Antarctic
Peninsula

Australian territory

Edge of ice shelf   Cape Horn

Australia in Antarctica

Location

Antarctica lies in the southern hemisphere below the latitude of 60°S and is 2000 kilometres due south from Melbourne. Mawson, Australia's first Antarctic station, is 5200 kilometres south-south-west of Perth.

Landform

Ice comprises more than 95 per cent of the total surface and the other 5 per cent is bare rock. The greatest rock exposures are in the Antarctic Peninsula and the Trans-Antarctic Mountains. Antarctica has enough ice to cover the whole of Australia with a mantle of snow nearly 2 kilometres thick.

Climate

Antarctica has one of the most hostile environments on earth. It experiences the coldest temperatures, the strongest winds and the largest deserts on earth. In coastal areas at 1000 metres, the mean annual temperature is minus 12°C, while in high parts, near 4000 metres, it falls to minus 60°C. The high plateau receives very little precipitation at all and is the world's largest and driest desert. A little more snow falls in the lower areas and is equivalent to an annual rainfall of 5 centimetres—half as much as is experienced by places like Birdsville, Queensland. The quantity of ice present has been formed by the accumulation of snow over millions of years.

In winter it is so cold that the surrounding sea freezes to 200–300 kilometres off shore and in summer the ice breaks to form pack ice. Under the influence of winds and tides it is distributed widely in the Southern Ocean exerting a major influence on the world's weather patterns. During mid-winter it experiences twenty-four hours of darkness and during mid-summer there are twenty-four hours of daylight.

Population

There are no permanent inhabitants but world scientists are continually studying this vast continent; few stay longer than two years.

Australia maintains four

DID YOU KNOW?
An international embargo on mineral exploration in the Antarctic will be enforced until the end of the century.

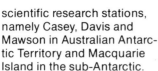

scientific research stations, namely Casey, Davis and Mawson in Australian Antarctic Territory and Macquarie Island in the sub-Antarctic.

Flora and fauna

Because of intense cold and dryness, only simple algae, lichens and mosses, and a few tiny animals, such as mites, live there the year round. Many birds and animals breed on the fringes of the continent during summer, but move northward for the winter. These include penguins, albatross, snow petrels, various species of seal and whales. The ocean around the Antarctic has a distinct fish fauna of some 100 species, 75 per cent of which are Antarctic 'cod' (not found in other seas) and hagfishes, skates, squid and small eel-pouts.

DID YOU KNOW?

Australia is one of the more ancient land masses in the world. For the past 80–90 million years, it has been free of major mountain building events, which makes it the most stable land mass in the world.

Australia in proportion to Europe

Australia's official name is the Commonwealth of Australia. Its form of government is a constitutional monarchy. The head of the state is Queen Elizabeth II of the United Kingdom of Great Britain and Northern Ireland, who is also Queen of Australia. She is represented in Australia by the governor-general. The head of government is the prime minister, leader of the party or coalition of parties holding a majority in the federal parliament.

Australia is an independent self-governing member of the British Commonwealth of Nations, and a foundation member of the United Nations. It is in alliance with the United States of America and New Zealand in the ANZUS pact, and a member of the South-East Asia Treaty Organisation (SEATO).

It is a federation of six states, with two internal federal territories—the Australian Capital Territory and the Northern Territory—and a number of external territories—Norfolk Island, Cocos Island, Christmas Island, Lord Howe Island, Macquarie Island, Australian Antarctica between 45° and 160° longitude—under its control.

Levels of government

Federal

Australia chose its executive form of government, consisting of a prime minister and cabinet, mainly from the British Westminster system. As well, some minor aspects of the United States congressional system were adopted.

The Australian federal parliament is generally responsible for matters of national importance. These include defence, external affairs, customs and excise, communications, foreign trade, social services, treasury, and immigration. In addition it shares mutual responsibilities with the state legislatures. These include education, agriculture, energy services, health, and law enforcement.

The Australian constitution, a document agreed to by the separate colonies in 1901 at federation, limits the power of the federal government. To maintain strict control, the constitution can be altered only by a referendum.

The Executive Council has the task of advising the governor-general, who presides over the formal processes that give cabinet decisions legal force. Major political decisions affecting the nation do not come from the governor-general, but from various meetings of cabinet members.

Not all ministers need be members of cabinet. The cabinet consists of leading figures of the governing party and the Senate (those with senior portfolios), with the prime minister as chairman. Junior ministers attend cabinet meetings only when matters affecting their departmental responsibilities are being discussed.

DID YOU KNOW?

Australia is the only English-speaking country to have made voting compulsory in federal and state elections. It results in a voter turn-out of 95 per cent.

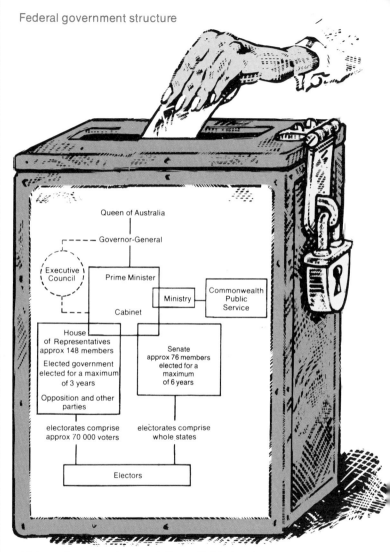

Queen of Australia

Governor-General

Executive Council

Prime Minister

Ministry

Commonwealth Public Service

Cabinet

House of Representatives approx 148 members

Elected government elected for a maximum of 3 years

Opposition and other parties

Senate approx 76 members elected for a maximum of 6 years

electorates comprise approx 70 000 voters

electorates comprise whole states

Electors

All Australians over the age of 18 are eligible to vote.
Voting is compulsory for everyone except Aboriginals. Aboriginals may choose whether or not to register; if they register, they must vote.

State

State governments are also modelled on the British Westminster system, each having a premier as leader of the cabinet and ministry.

The state parliaments deal with domestic affairs, such as housing, trade, education, industry and law enforcement within the states, as well as sharing mutual responsibilities with the federal parliament.

Local

The *Local Government Act* was passed in 1919. This gave power to areas as small as cities, municipalities and shires, to provide a more satisfactory system of government within the local area with a mayor or president as leader. Australia has 900 bodies at local government level. They have varying responsibilities which may include urban planning, road construction, water, sewerage and drainage, and local community activities.

Voting

Compulsory preferential voting is the most common system used in Australia. In voting for the House of Representatives, one candidate only from any one party is selected to represent each electorate. The voter must vote for all the candidates in order of preference. If no candidate receives an absolute majority, then there is a distribution of preference votes.

The number of members of the House of Representatives depends on the population of each state. In 1987 there were 148 members: fifty-one for New South Wales; thirty-nine for Victoria; twenty-four for Queensland; thirteen for South Australia; thirteen for Western Australia; five for Tasmania; two for the Australian Capital Territory; and one for the Northern Territory.

Proportional representation is the other major electoral system in Australia. It is used in the Senate and in some state elections. Each Senator represents a whole state; as the electorate is so large, more than one candidate is elected for each state. In 1987 there were 76 senators; twelve for each state, and two for each territory.

State governments

Each state except the Northern
Territory has an executive council
consisting of the governor,
premier and selected ministers.

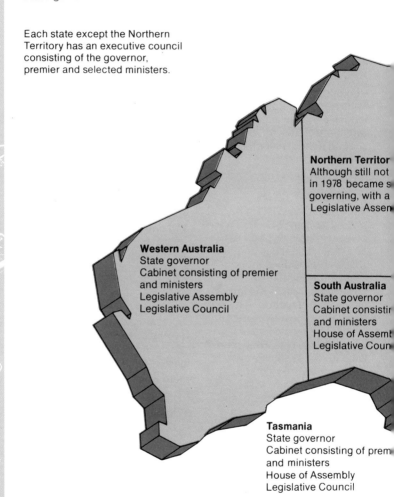

Northern Territor
Although still not
in 1978 became s
governing, with a
Legislative Assen

Western Australia
State governor
Cabinet consisting of premier
and ministers
Legislative Assembly
Legislative Council

South Australia
State governor
Cabinet consistir
and ministers
House of Assemb
Legislative Coun

Tasmania
State governor
Cabinet consisting of prem
and ministers
House of Assembly
Legislative Council

DID YOU KNOW?
The world's largest electorate (2 255 278 square
kilometres) is Kalgoorlie, Western Australia.

Federal parliament

A *double dissolution* of parliament is the dissolving of both the House of Representatives and the Senate due to a deadlock arising over the passing of a bill. This necessitates a general election of both houses.

The unusual procedure of a *joint sitting* of parliament occurs when a party wins a majority in the House of Representatives but not in the Senate, after a double dissolution. Both the House of Representatives and the Senate may sit jointly to work out a solution if a deadlock still exists.

Supply is the money granted by the passing of legislation before the end of the financial year in order to proceed until the next budget is passed. *Appropriation bills* authorise the use of revenue collected by the government.

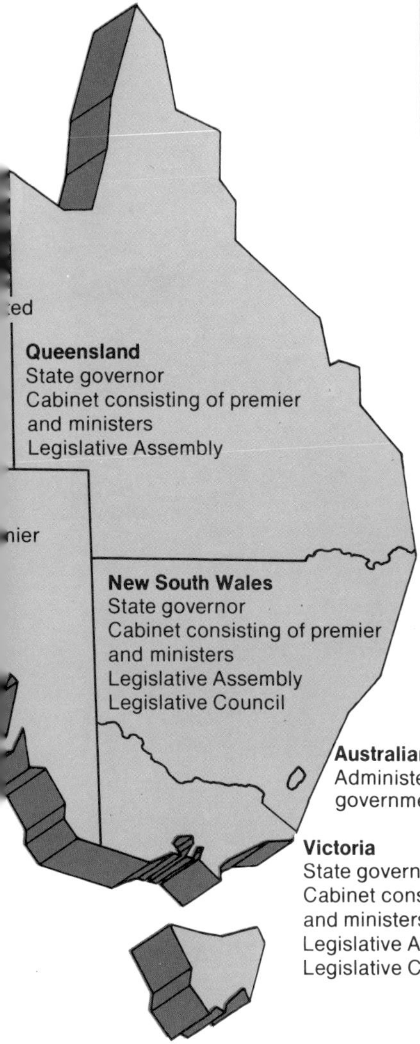

ed

Queensland
State governor
Cabinet consisting of premier
and ministers
Legislative Assembly

nier

New South Wales
State governor
Cabinet consisting of premier
and ministers
Legislative Assembly
Legislative Council

Australian Capital Territory
Administered by the federal
government

Victoria
State governor
Cabinet consisting of premier
and ministers
Legislative Assembly
Legislative Council

Local government structure

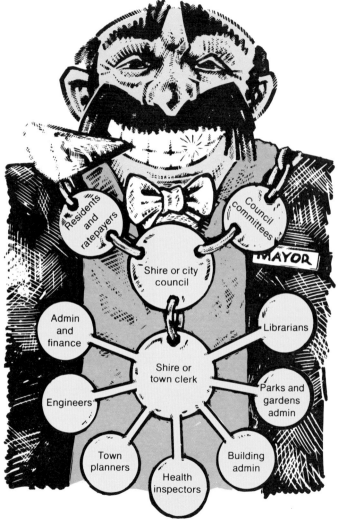

Residents and ratepayers
Council committees
MAYOR
Shire or city council
Admin and finance
Librarians
Shire or town clerk
Engineers
Parks and gardens admin
Town planners
Health inspectors
Building admin

Voting is compulsory in some states

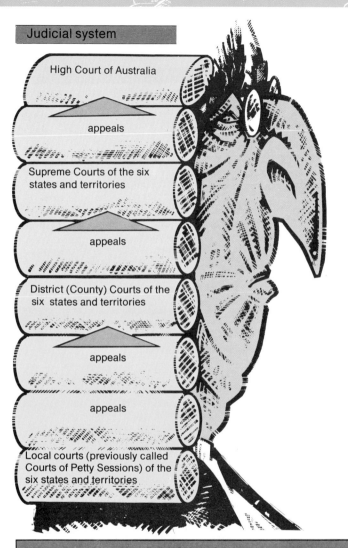

Judicial system

High Court of Australia

appeals

Supreme Courts of the six states and territories

appeals

District (County) Courts of the six states and territories

appeals

appeals

Local courts (previously called Courts of Petty Sessions) of the six states and territories

DID YOU KNOW

There are approximately 175 local courts in each state which deal with 98 per cent of all cases heard in Australia.

Payments, purchases, production

The Australian economy follows the system of 'free enterprise', although this is moderated by protective tariff barriers (particularly in vehicle-building, footwear, clothing and textiles) and 'orderly marketing' of most agricultural products.

Income and expenditure

The federal and state governments have separate areas of responsibility for raising and spending revenue.

The financial year begins on 1 July.

Floating of the Australian dollar

In December 1983 the Government decided to allow the Australian Dollar to *float*, that is, to establish its value in the foreign exchange market by the process of supply and demand. Prior to this the Reserve Bank set the value for the Australian dollar against the U.S. dollar, on a daily basis.

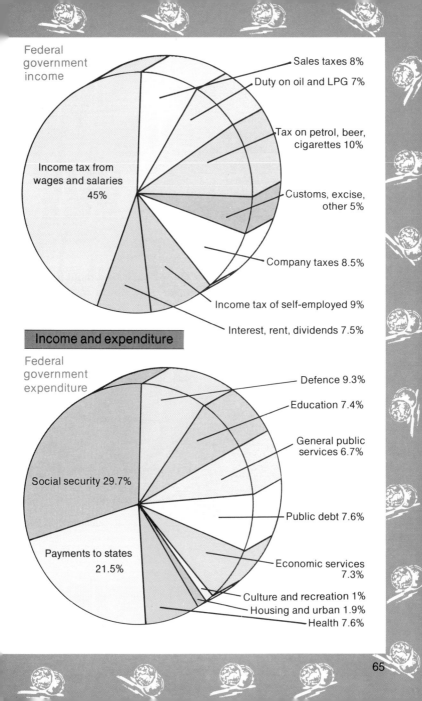

Federal government income

Sales taxes 8%

Duty on oil and LPG 7%

Tax on petrol, beer, cigarettes 10%

Income tax from wages and salaries 45%

Customs, excise, other 5%

Company taxes 8.5%

Income tax of self-employed 9%

Interest, rent, dividends 7.5%

Income and expenditure

Federal government expenditure

Defence 9.3%

Education 7.4%

General public services 6.7%

Social security 29.7%

Public debt 7.6%

Payments to states 21.5%

Economic services 7.3%

Culture and recreation 1%

Housing and urban 1.9%

Health 7.6%

Basket of currencies — Trade Weighted Index

The *Trade Weighted Index* (TWI) is a measure of performance of the value of the Australian dollar against a 'basket' of such currencies as the US dollar, Japanese yen, English pound, Deutsche mark, New Zealand dollar, etc. These are weighted in percentage terms to approximately the value of each country's trade with Australia.

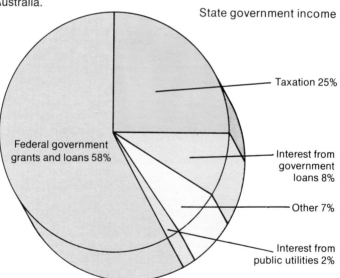

State government income

Taxation 25%

Federal government grants and loans 58%

Interest from government loans 8%

Other 7%

Interest from public utilities 2%

Federal versus state expenditure

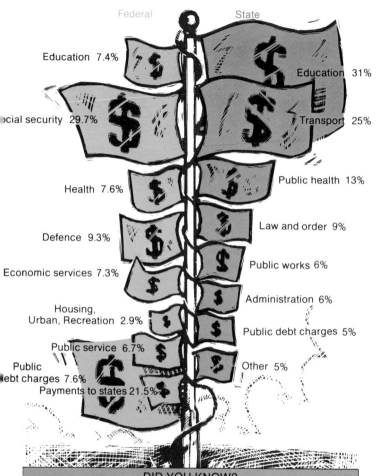

Federal

Education 7.4%

ocial security 29.7%

Health 7.6%

Defence 9.3%

Economic services 7.3%

Housing,
Urban, Recreation 2.9%

Public service 6.7%

Public
ebt charges 7.6%

Payments to states 21.5%

State

Education 31%

Transport 25%

Public health 13%

Law and order 9%

Public works 6%

Administration 6%

Public debt charges 5%

Other 5%

DID YOU KNOW?

The first ration list, per person per week, was issued by Governor Philip in 1788. It included 7 lbs (3.17 kg) of either bread or flour; 7 lbs of beef or 4 lbs (1.81 kg) of pork; 3 lbs (1.36 kg) of peas; 6 oz (0.170 kg) of butter, and $\frac{1}{2}$ lb (250 g) of rice.

Average weekly earnings

1919
$6.00

1948
$11.60

1970
$76.00

1975
$148.00

1980
$247.60

1982
$307.00

1986
$418.90

DID YOU KNOW?
The highest paid jobs for males are in the mining industry;
for females, in community services (health, education,
etc.).

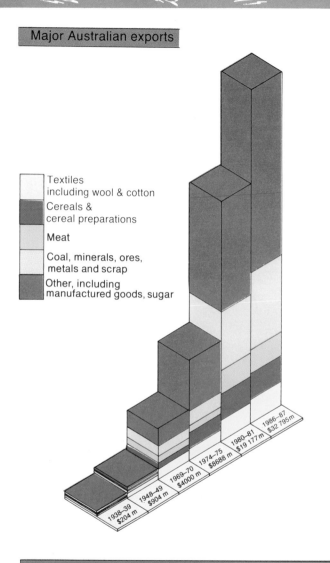

Major Australian exports

Textiles including wool & cotton

Cereals & cereal preparations

Meat

Coal, minerals, ores, metals and scrap

Other, including manufactured goods, sugar

1938–39 $204 m

1948–49 $904 m

1969–70 $4000 m

1974–75 $8688 m

1980–81 $19 177 m

1986–87 $32 795m

DID YOU KNOW?
New South Wales did not succeed in growing enough wheat to feed its inhabitants until 1900.

Exports 1986
Total $32 795.4 m

EXPORTS
1986

Japan $9 350.0 m
EEC $4 634.0 m
USA $3 257.4 m
ASEAN $2 137.3 m
NZ $1 508.6 m
China, Republic of $1 497.3 m
Korea, Republic of $1 317.1 m
Taiwan $1 064.3 m
USSR $969.7 m

Imports 1986
Total $34 667.1 m

IMPORTS 1986

EEC $8 383.8 m
Japan $8 248.2 m
USA $7 284.8 m
ASEAN $1 603.3 m
NZ $1 454.5 m
Taiwan $1 116.1 m
Korea $556.6 m
China, Republic of $435.02 m
USSR $10.2 m

70

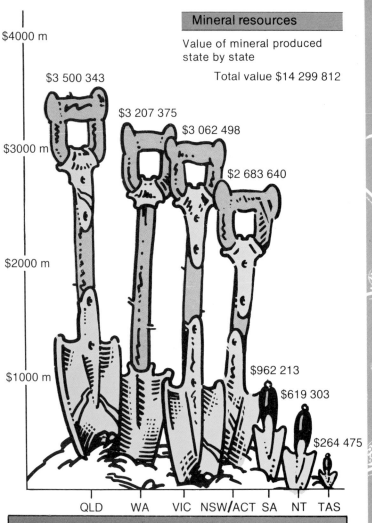

Mineral resources

Value of mineral produced
state by state

Total value $14 299 812

$4000 m

$3 500 343

$3 207 375

$3 062 498

$2 683 640

$3000 m

$2000 m

$962 213

$619 303

$1000 m

$264 475

QLD   WA   VIC   NSW/ACT   SA   NT   TAS

DID YOU KNOW?

Between the towns of Ooldia and Nurina in Western
Australia, is the world's longest straight stretch of railway,
478.4 kilometres in length.

Australia's mineral resources

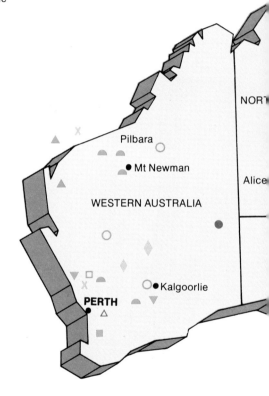

- □ Silver, Lead, Zinc
- ▲ Oil
- ✕ Gas
- △ Bauxite
- ■ Coal
- ○ Gold
- ◖ Iron ore
- ◈ Uranium
- ● Copper
- ▼ Nickel

Pilbara

● Mt Newman

WESTERN AUSTRALIA

NORT

Alice

○ ● Kalgoorlie

PERTH

DID YOU KNOW?
Australia's three main opal fields are in Quilpie,
Queensland, Lightning Ridge, New South Wales, and
Coober Pedy, South Australia.

RITORY

△

□

Mt Isa

QUEENSLAND

USTRALIA

BRISBANE

Broken Hill

NEW SOUTH WALES

ADELAIDE

SYDNEY

Canberra

VICTORIA

MELBOURNE

Launceston

TASMANIA

HOBART

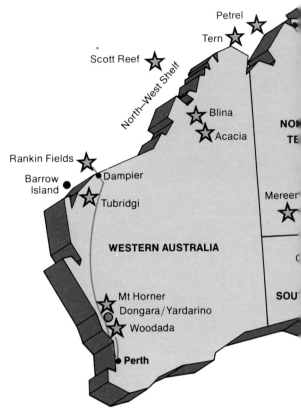

Australia's oil and gas fields

Petrel

Tern

Scott Reef

North–West Shelf

Blina

Acacia

NORTHERN TERRITORY

Rankin Fields

Barrow Island

Dampier

Tubridgi

Mereenie

WESTERN AUSTRALIA

Mt Horner

Dongara/Yardarino

Woodada

SOUTH

Perth

- ◯ Oil and gas producer
- ◎ Gas producer
- ☆ Oil or gas discovery, possibly commercial
- ▪ Major oil shale deposit
- ___ Gas pipeline
- .... Oil pipeline
- _ _ Proposed pipeline

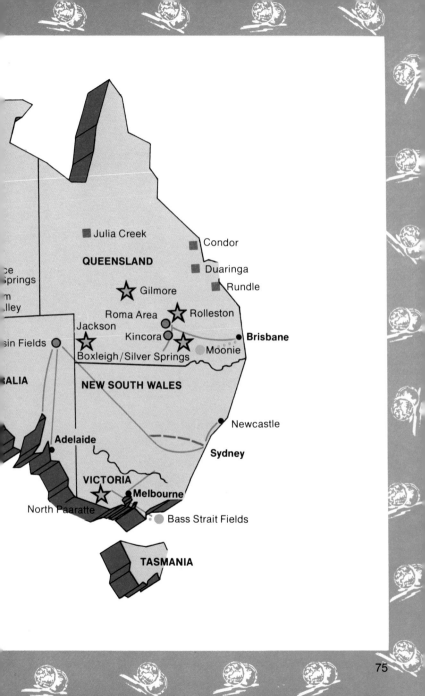

Julia Creek

QUEENSLAND

Condor

Duaringa

Rundle

Gilmore

Roma Area
Jackson

Rolleston

Kincora

Brisbane

Boxleigh/Silver Springs

Moonie

NEW SOUTH WALES

Newcastle

Adelaide

Sydney

VICTORIA

Melbourne

North Paaratte

Bass Strait Fields

TASMANIA

ce
prings

lley

sin Fields

ALIA

75

Comparative graph—value of minerals produced 1980—85

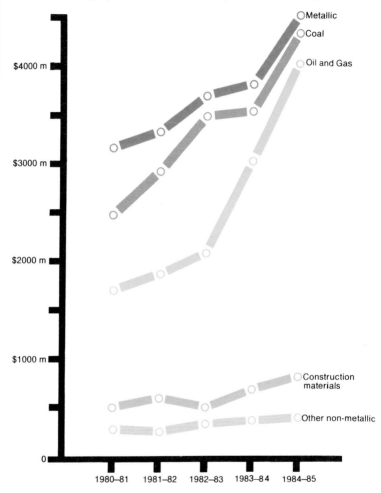

DID YOU KNOW?
Sydney Harbour, or Port Jackson, extends over 55
square kilometres.

Currency

Until 1966, Australia followed the British system of currency at that time, which was pounds, shillings and pence. Decimal currency was introduced on 14 February 1966, the dollar ($A) being the unit of currency and consisting of 100 cents. The notes show famous people and the coins depict animals.

Coins

The bronze one-cent coin depicts the nocturnal feathertail glider, Australia's smallest possum. The bronze two-cent coin depicts the frill-necked lizard, found in Australia's tropical north. The lizard's one-metre length is mostly tail. The bronze in the coins comprises 97 per cent copper, 2.5 per cent zinc and 0.5 per cent tin. The other coins (with the exception of the $1, $10 and $200) are cupro-nickel, which is 75 per cent copper and 25 per cent nickel.

The five-cent piece shows the echidna or spiny ant-eater. The echidna is one of only two egg-laying mammals, both of which are native to Australia. The ten-cent coin shows a male lyrebird dancing and singing, its magnificent tail expanded and thrown forward over its head. The twenty-cent piece

presents the only other egg-laying mammal, the platypus, which is found in waterways on the east of the continent. The standard fifty-cent piece carries the arms of the Commonwealth of Australia, supported by a kangaroo and an emu. The coin is used for commemorative purposes and is frequently minted with a special design.

The aluminium-bronze $1 coin portrays five kangaroos on the reverse. It features interrupted milling on the edge to assist visually impaired people. Commemorative $10 and $200 dollar coins are not widely circulated. The $10 coin has been issued only once, in 1982, on the occasion of the Brisbane Commonwealth Games. It is made of 92.5 per cent silver and 7.5 per cent copper. The $200 coin, which is 22-carat gold, was first minted in 1980.

Banknotes

The currency has six notes, each increasing in size with its value and all depicting personalities of Australian historical interest.

$2 note

The $2 note commemorates John Macarthur, who made a major contribution to the development of Australia's early wool industry by successfully breeding fine-wool merino sheep and pioneering the export of wool to Britain.

The reverse side commemorates William Farrer whose pioneering work in developing new wheat strains helped establish the Australian wheat industry.

$5 note

The $5 note honours Sir Joseph Banks, famed botanist, who accompanied James Cook. The banksia plant is named after him. His portrait on the note is flanked by a collection of Australian native plants.

The back carries a likeness of Mrs Caroline Chisholm, who showed a compassionate interest in destitute women when they arrived in the colony of New South Wales without work or lodging during the early days of settlement.

$10 note

The $10 note commemorates Francis Greenway, the convict who became Australia's first civil architect. He designed some of the colony's early public buildings, including the Hyde Park Barracks and St James Church in Sydney.

Henry Lawson, who captured the spirit of much of the early life of Australia in his writings, including the humour, hardships and

sometimes rugged conditions, is portrayed on the back of the note, where some of his handwriting is reproduced.

$20 note

The $20 note features pioneer aviator Sir Charles Kingsford Smith, who made the first trans-Pacific flight from San Francisco to Brisbane in the monoplane *Southern Cross*.

Another aeronautical pioneer, Lawrence Hargrave, backs the note, together with copies of his drawings of flying-machines and kites. (The originals are held in Sydney's Museum of Applied Arts and Sciences.) Hargrave's research into flying-machines contributed to the development of flying early this century.

$50 note

The $50 note portrays Nobel Prize winner Howard Florey, an experimental pathologist occurring anti-bacterial substances led to his part in discovering the clinical value of penicillin and other antibiotics.

Lord Florey's fellow-scientist Sir Ian Clunies-Ross, renowned for his work on parasites affecting livestock and his long association with the Australian Commonwealth Scientific and Industrial Research Organisation (now the CSIRO), is pictured on the back of the note.

$100 note

The $100 note has the famous Antarctic explorer and geologist Sir Douglas Mawson on the front.

John Tebbutt, the astronomer, compiled astronomical and meteorological observations which helped lay the foundations of astronomy in Australia. His image is on the back of the note.

DID YOU KNOW?

Sydney Harbour Bridge has an arch span of 503 metres. The top arch is 134 metres above sea level. Overall length of arch and approaches is 1149 metres, with a deck width of 49 metres. The bridge weighs approximately 52 800 tonnes and the weight of the steel in the arch is 39 000 tonnes.

Australian Capital Territory

Jervis Bay

Two areas transferred to the Commonwealth of Australia by the state of New South Wales make up the Australian Capital Territory. In 1908 the larger area around Canberra was chosen for the federal capital site and in 1915 the smaller area Jervis Bay on the New South Wales south coast was transferred to the Commonwealth of Australia. The seat of government was moved from Melbourne to Canberra in 1927.

Location

The greater part of the Australian Capital Territory is in south-eastern New South Wales, west of the Great Dividing Range. The smaller, Jervis Bay area is on the New South Wales Southern coast.

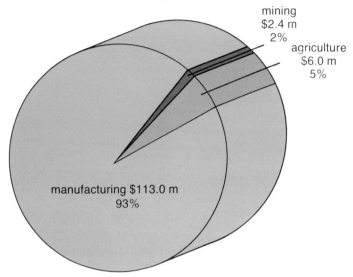

Australian Capital Territory—gross value of production

mining
$2.4 m
2%

agriculture
$6.0 m
5%

manufacturing $113.0 m
93%

Area

The area around Canberra is 2400 square kilometres and Jervis Bay consists of 73 square kilometres.

Landform

Rolling plains and grasslands. Gentle slopes and coastal plains in Jervis Bay area.

Population

249 400 mostly residents of Canberra.

Climate

Mainly temperate — cold nights and cool to very cold days in winter, warm to hot days and cool nights in summer. Slightly humid in coastal areas.

Administrative centre

Canberra is situated at the northern end of the Australian Capital Territory. It has an area of 805 square kilometres and has a population of 248 400, of which 28 per cent are public servants. Average daily hours of sunshine, 7.2.

Main attractions

Parliament House, Lake Burley Griffin, High Courts of Australia, Captain Cook Water Spout, Red Hill, Black Mountain, Telecom Tower, American War Memorial, Australian War Museum, foreign legations, Yarralumla (governor-general's residence).

Major festivals

March	Canberra Festival
June	Canberra Festival of Drama
	Canberra Embassies' Open Day
October	Canberra Oktoberfest
November	Canberra Spring Flower Show
December	Canberra Australian Lithuanian Festival

Canberra from the air showing the new Parliament House in the centre.

DID YOU KNOW?

The plan for Canberra was the work of an American, Walter Burley Griffin (1876–1937), who also designed a number of notable buildings throughout Australia. Griffin planned the development and many of the homes of Castlecrag, a Sydney suburb with extensive harbour views.

New South Wales

Location

NSW lies in the south-east of the continent on the Pacific Ocean, with Queensland to the north and Victoria to the south.

Area

It is the fourth-largest state in Australia and is 801 600 square kilometres (seven times larger than England).

Landform

Coastal slopes, plateaus and river flats are bounded by the Great Dividing Range which runs north and south. West of the Dividing Range are rolling plains which deteriorate into semi-arid desert.

Population

5 543 500. The majority of people live in the three main cities — Sydney, Newcastle, and Wollongong. More than half the people of the state live in Sydney.

Climate

Temperate and slightly humid in coastal areas with the deserts of the interior experiencing cold nights and hot days. Irregular floods and droughts occur.

State capital

Sydney is built on Port Jackson, a sea inlet on the Pacific Ocean. The city has an area of 12 407 square kilometres (including Penrith and Gosford) and a population of 3 391 600. Average daily hours of sunshine, 6.7.

New South Wales animal emblem: platypus

New South Wales floral emblem: waratah

DID YOU KNOW?

Up until 1902 there were laws in force preventing bathing in the daytime on inner city beaches.

New South Wales—gross value of production

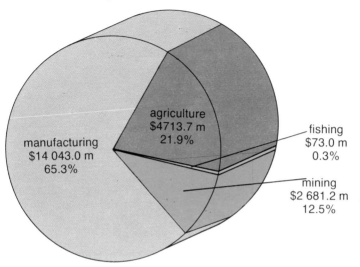

manufacturing
$14 043.0 m
65.3%

agriculture
$4713.7 m
21.9%

fishing
$73.0 m
0.3%

mining
$2 681.2 m
12.5%

Largest cities

Sydney (3 391 600)
Newcastle (423 300)
Wollongong (236 800)
Wagga Wagga (50 100)
Albury (45 250)
Tamworth (33 600)
Broken Hill (26 950)

Chief products

Manufacturing:

Agricultural implements, chemicals, clothing, fertiliser, glassware, iron and steel, machinery, motor cars, paper, textiles.

Mining:

Asbestos, coal, copper, gold, lead, mineral sands, silver, zinc.

Agricultural:

Dairy products, cotton, fruit, honey, mutton, poultry, sugar, wheat, wool, timber.

Fishing:

Many varieties of fish and shellfish.

Main attractions

Sydney Harbour Bridge, Opera House, Blue Mountains, Murrumbidgee irrigation area, Snowy Mountains, national parks, surfing beaches, fishing, wineries. Sometimes known as 'The Premier State'.

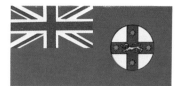
New South Wales flag

New South Wales coat of arms

Flag

The New South Wales flag is based on the Blue Ensign with the state badge superimposed on the right-hand side. The badge consists of a golden lion on a red St George Cross within a white circle. This badge was proclaimed in 1876.

Coat of arms

The present coat of arms was approved in 1906 by King Edward VII. It consists of a shield with the red cross of St George. In the quarters are displayed sheaves of wheat and fleece from the sheep, representing the agricultural and pastoral industries of the state. The shield is supported by a lion and a kangaroo. The crest is a rising sun with rays, each tagged with the flame of fire. The scroll at the base bears the motto, *Orta recens quam pura nites* (Newly arisen, how brightly you shine).

Sydney Opera House

Major festivals

January	Festival of Sydney
March	Orange Festival of Arts
April	Albury Heritage Week
	Bathurst Grand Prix Motor-Bike Races
	Tumut Festival of the Fallen Leaf
May	Coonabarabran Chrysanthemum Show
August	Wagga Wagga School of Arts Drama Festival
	Leeton Citrus Festival
	Lightning Ridge Opal Festival
	Newcastle Mattara Festival
September	Bowral Tulip Time
	Tuncurry and Forster Great Lakes Oyster Festival
	Gosford Festival of the Waters
	Goulburn Lilac Time Festival
October	Bathurst James Hardie 1000 Car Race
	Grafton Jacaranda Festival
	Tamworth Australian Country Music Star Maker Quest
November	Blackheath Rhododendron Festival
	Glen Innes The Land of the Beardies Bush Festival
December	Berrima Arts Festival
	Stroud Charity Carnival

Sister cities

Coffs Harbour	Hayama (Japan)
Cooma	Kamoto-cho (Japan)
Lismore	Yamato-takada (Japan)
Manly	Taito-ku, Tokyo (Japan)
Newcastle	Arcadia (USA)
	Ube (Japan)
Orange	Kofu (Japan)
Sydney	Nagoya (Japan)
	San Francisco (USA)
	Wellington (New Zealand)
	Portsmouth (United Kingdom)
	Guangzhou (People's Republic of China)
Wollongong	Kimitsu (Japan)

Victoria

Location
Victoria lies in the south-eastern corner of the continent.

Area
It is the smallest state on the mainland and is 227 600 square kilometres in area.

Landform
Mountainous areas in the north-east, and semi-desert areas in north-west. Most land is well suited to farming and as a result Victoria is often referred to as 'The Garden State'.

Population
4 164 700. Victoria is the most densely populated and most highly urbanised of all the states.

Climate
Generally temperate, although the climate is subject to wide variation. High rainfall, extremes of summer heat and irregular floods and droughts occur.

State capital
Melbourne is situated on the Yarra River, at Port Phillip Bay. It has an area of 6109 square kilometres and a population of 2 916 600 (seven-tenths of the state's population). Melbourne's motto is *Vires acquirit eundo*, meaning 'We gather strength as we grow'. Average daily hours of sunshine, 5.7.

Largest cities
Melbourne (2 916 600)
Geelong and environs (147 070)
Ballarat (77 500)
Bendigo (63 730)
Shepparton (26 240)

Victorian floral emblem: pink heath

Victorian animal emblem: Leadbeater's possum

Victoria—gross value of production

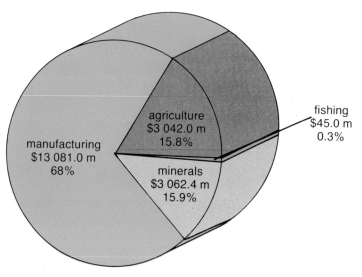

- manufacturing $13 081.0 m 68%
- agriculture $3 042.0 m 15.8%
- minerals $3 062.4 m 15.9%
- fishing $45.0 m 0.3%

Chief products

Agricultural:

Cattle, forest products, fruit, hay, straw, milk, dairy products, poultry, eggs, sheep, vegetables, wheat and wool.

Manufacturing:

Building materials, chemical products, clothing, farm machinery, footwear, textiles, light engineering and motor vehicles.

Mining:

Brown coal, natural gas, oil.

Main attractions

Melbourne Cup (began 1861), Australian Rules Football, wineries, prospecting, river boat cruising, surfing, snowfields, national parks, sailing, fishing. Educational system, cultural institutions and communications media are well advanced.

DID YOU KNOW?
During the depression (1929–32), one wage earner in four was 'on the dole' (unemployment benefit).

Flag

Victoria was the first state to have its own flag. The flag is made up of the Blue Ensign with the badge of the state. This consists of five white stars of the Southern Cross in the fly above which is a crown. It was used as early as 1870.

Victorian flag

Coat of arms

The present coat of arms was granted by Queen Elizabeth II in 1972. It incorporates a shield with five stars representing the constellation of the Southern Cross. On either side stands a female figure, one representing peace and the other representing prosperity. The figure of peace is holding an olive branch and the figure of

Victorian coat of arms

prosperity is holding a cornucopia, or horn of plenty. The crest consists of a kangaroo, bearing in its paws an Imperial Crown. Below the shield is the motto, 'Peace and prosperity'.

Paddle steamer on the Murray River

Major festivals

January/ February	Cobram Peaches and Cream Festival (bi-annual)
March	Melbourne Moomba Festival
	Ballarat Begonia Festival
Easter	Bendigo Easter Fair
	Beechworth Golden Horseshoes Easter Festival
	Stawell Gift (Easter Monday)
April/May	Bright's Autumn Festival
June	Echuca Steam Rally
September/ October	Halls Gap Wildflower Exhibition
October	Benalla Rose Festival
	Euroa Wool Week
	Hamilton Heritage Festival
	Mildura Bottlebrush Festival
	Dandenong Tulip Festival
November	Melbourne Cup
	Melbourne Lygon Street Festa
	Melbourne Oktoberfest
	Mansfield Mountain Country Festival

Sister cities

Altona	Anjo (Japan)
Box Hill	Matsudo (Japan)
Frankston	Suson (Japan)
Melbourne	Osaka (Japan)
	Boston (USA)
	Tianjin (China)
	Thessalonika (Greece)
	Florence (Italy)
Portland	Uchiura-cho (Japan)
Shepparton	Esashi (Japan)
Swan Hill	Yamagata (Japan)
Warrnambool	Miura (Japan)
Yarrawonga	Katsuyama-mura (Japan)

DID YOU KNOW?
In 1854 a large meteorite was found at Cranbourne,
Victoria, weighing more than 5 tonnes.

Queensland

Location

Queensland lies on the north-east of the continent, bordering the Pacific Ocean to the east, and the Torres Strait to the north.

Area

Second-largest state in Australia; 1 727 200 square kilometres.

Landform

The north coast is sheltered by islands and the Great Barrier Reef system. Behind the coastal slopes of the Great Dividing Range and river flats, are rolling plains. Then the land becomes semi-arid desert.

Population

2 592 600, mostly in four coastal areas.

Climate

The climate is mostly tropical, with two main seasons: wet and dry. Queensland is known as 'The Sunshine State' because of pleasantly warm winters and long hours of sunshine.

State capital

Brisbane, situated on Brisbane River on east coast. It has an area of 3080 square kilometres, and a population of 1 157 000. Average daily hours of sunshine, 7.5.

Largest cities

Brisbane (1 157 200)
Gold Coast (208 100)
Townsville (101 700)
Cairns (67 370)
Rockhampton (57 020)
Mackay (49 040)
Mt Isa (24 440)

Queensland animal emblem: koala

Queensland floral emblem: Cooktown orchid

Queensland—gross value of production

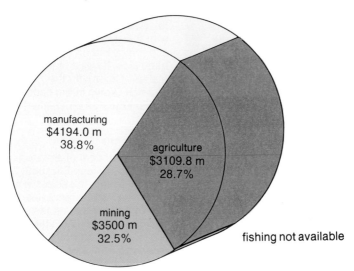

manufacturing
$4194.0 m
38.8%

agriculture
$3109.8 m
28.7%

mining
$3500 m
32.5%

fishing not available

Chief products

Agriculture:

Barley, cotton, fruit, maize, wheat, peanuts, sugar, tobacco, pigs, sheep, cattle.

Manufacturing:

Meat products, aerated waters, dairy products, brick making, timber and log processing, ready mixed concrete, electricity generation, basic metal products.

Mining:

Bauxite, coal, copper, gold, lead, mineral sands, nickel, salt, tin, uranium, zinc.

Main attractions

The Great Barrier Reef (a complex organic system and one of the greatest biological wonders of the world), surfing beaches, fishing, palm-fringed coastline, tropical islands, prospecting, national parks, tropical rainforests.

DID YOU KNOW?
The Great Barrier Reef is the longest coral reef in the world, extending over 2012.5 kilometres.

Queensland flag

:: AUDAX · AT · FIDELIS ::

Queensland coat of arms

Flag

The flag of Queensland is based on the Blue Ensign with the state badge superimposed on the right-hand side. It has a blue Maltese Cross with the Imperial Crown in the centre. This badge was proclaimed in 1876.

Coat of arms

The present coat of arms was granted by Queen Elizabeth II in 1977. Within the shield is a bull's head and a ram's head in profile representing the pastoral industry. Also there is a mound of quartz emerging from a golden pyramid, in front of which is a spade and pick representing the mining industry. In the other quarter is a sheaf of wheat representing the agricultural industry. The shield is supported by a red deer and a brolga. The crest comprises the Maltese Cross superimposed by the Imperial Crown. These are held between two stalks of sugar cane. At the base is the motto, *Audax at fidelis* (Bold-aye-but faithful too.)

DID YOU KNOW?
Tully in Queensland is the wettest town in Australia with an average annual rainfall of 355.6 centimetres.

Major festivals

January	Clermont Beef 'n' Beer Festival
May	Dimbulah Tobacco Festival
June	Brisbane Festival of Creative Arts
July	Thursday Island Coming of the Light Festival
September	Maryborough Spring Festival
	Mackay Sugartime Festival
	Stradbroke Island Wildflower Festival
	Toowoomba Carnival of Flowers
October	Warana Festival
	Ipswich Country Music Festival
	Bundaberg Harvest Festival
	Rockhampton Rocktoberfest
	Cairns Fun in the Sun Festival
	Coolangatta Tropicarnival
	Gympie Gold Rush Festival
November	Yeppoon Pineapple Festival
December	Beaudesert Lions' Christmas Carnival

Sister cities

Brisbane	Brisbane, California (USA)
Cairns	Hiwasa-cho (Japan)
Rockhampton	Ibusuki (Japan)

Great Barrier Reef

South Australia

Location

South Australia occupies a central position on the southern coastline. Seaward is the Great Australian Bight.

Area

It is the third-largest state and covers one-eighth of the total area of Australia. It is 984 000 square kilometres in area with a coastline of 3700 kilometres.

Landform

Undulating hills, grasslands and valleys. Semi-arid desert to the north.

Population

Sparsely populated, with 1 373 100 people, mainly concentrated in the south-east corner of the state.

Climate

Mostly a mediterranean climate, warm to hot in summer and cool in winter. It is the driest state, with four-fifths of its total area receiving less than 254 millimetres of rainfall a year.

State capital

Adelaide, situated on the Torrens River in St Vincent Gulf, is sheltered by Mount Lofty Range. The population is 987 100 and its area is 1870 square kilometres. Average daily hours of sunshine, 6.9.

Largest cities and towns

Adelaide (987 100)
Elizabeth (31 980)
Whyalla (29 290)
Mt Gambier (19 270)
Port Augusta (16 290)
Port Pirie (15 690)

South Australian animal emblem: hairy-nosed wombat

South Australian floral emblem: Sturt's desert pea

South Australia—gross value of production

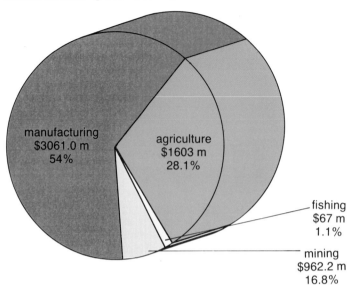

manufacturing
$3061.0 m
54%

agriculture
$1603 m
28.1%

fishing
$67 m
1.1%

mining
$962.2 m
16.8%

Chief products

Agricultural:

Almonds, barley, beef, dairy products, fruits, vegetables, wheat, wine, and wool.

Manufacturing:

Carriages and wagons, chemicals, cotton, electrical goods, iron and steel, machinery, pipes, motor cars.

Mining:

Barytes, coal, dolomite, gypsum, iron ore, natural gas, opals, salt, talc, copper.

Main attractions

Vineyards in Barossa Valley, Flinders Ranges, opal fields, Blue Lake—Mt Gambier, Kangaroo Island, Moonta and Burra Burra copper mine sites, The Barrages at Goolwa, Victor Harbour, Grand Prix.

DID YOU KNOW?
The Murray River flows with its own current through Lake Alexandrina, South Australia, on its course to its mouth at the Southern Ocean.

South Australian flag

South Australian coat of arms

Flag

The flag of South Australia is based on the Blue Ensign and has the badge of the state superimposed on the right-hand side. It consists of a piping shrike with wings outstretched, on a yellow background. This was adopted in 1904.

Coat of arms

The present coat of arms was conferred by Queen Elizabeth II in 1984. It incorporates a shield with a piping shrike displayed standing on the branch of a gum tree. The shield is supported on a grassy mound from which two vines grow entwining the stakes of the shield; on either side, stalks of wheat and barley appear; lying on the mound are two cog wheels and a miner's pick. All these represent aspects of industry in South Australia. Above the shield is a crest of four sprigs of Sturt's desert pea, and at the base is a scroll with the words 'South Australia'.

DID YOU KNOW?

The Great Artesian Basin is the largest in the world, with an area of 1 716 200 square kilometres. It stretches from south-west Queensland and north-west New South Wales into the Northern Territory and South Australia. Artesian water occurs over 60 per cent of the continent.

Major festivals

January	Hahndorf German Shooting Festival
	Tanunda Oom-pah Festival
February	Mt Gambier Italian Festival
March	Adelaide Festival of Arts (in even-numbered years)
	Adelaide Glendi Festival
	Tanunda Essenfest
Easter	Clare Valley Wine Festival (in even-numbered years)
April	Barossa Valley Vintage Festival (in odd-numbered years)
	Kapunda Celtic Music Festival
May	Adelaide Creative Arts Festival for the Young
	Melrose Mountain Fun Festival
	Moonta Cornish Festival
July	Willunga Almond Blossom Festival
October	Coober Pedy Outback Festival
	Murray Bridge Sagra Festival
	Grand Prix
	Victor Harbour Heritage Festival
November	Adelaide Christmas Pageant
December	Adelaide Christmas Earth Fair

Sister cities

Adelaide	Himeji (Japan)
	Austin (Texas, USA)
	Christchurch (New Zealand)
	Georgetown (Penang, Malaysia)

Festival Theatre, Adelaide

Western Australia

Western Australia occupies the western third of continent, bordered by the Indian Ocean in the west and the Southern Ocean in the south.

Area

It is the largest state in Australia, and is 2 525 500 square kilometres in area.

Landform

The state extends from vast arable southern areas to interior semi-desert landscapes and the mineral-rich Great Sandy and Gibson deserts to the north. The mountain ranges are Stirling, Kimberley and Hamersley ranges.

Population

1 440 600 (concentrated on south-west coast), representing only 8 per cent of the total Australian population.
The large desert and semi-desert areas are unsuitable for cultivation or close settlement.

Climate

Western Australia has three broad climate divisions. The northern part is tropical, receiving heavy rainfall. The south-west corner has a mediterranean climate, with long hot summers and wet winters. The remainder is mostly arid land or desert.

State capital

Perth, situated on the Swan River on the seaboard of the Indian Ocean. It is 5306 square kilometres in area and has a population of 1 001 000. Average daily hours of sunshine, 7.9.

Largest cities

Perth (1 001 000)
Bunbury (24 510)
Fremantle (23 590)
Geraldton (20 060)
Albany (14 050)
Port Hedland (14 210)
Boulder (12 240)
Kalgoorlie (10 390)

Western Australian animal emblem: numbat

Western Australian floral emblem: red and green kangaroo paw

Western Australia—gross value of production

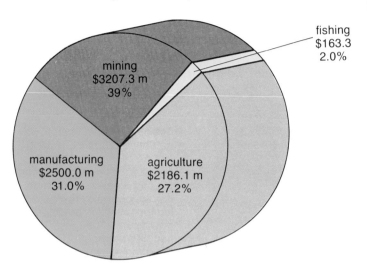

mining
$3207.3 m
39%

fishing
$163.3
2.0%

manufacturing
$2500.0 m
31.0%

agriculture
$2186.1 m
27.2%

Chief products

Agricultural:

Cattle, fruit, hardwoods, rock lobsters, wheat, wool.

Mining:

Bauxite, gold, ilmenite, iron ore, nickel, oil, salt.

Manufacturing:

Building materials, food and drink, metal, other mineral products, machinery, petroleum products, wood products.

Main attractions

Nullarbor Plain, Kalgoorlie goldfields, Esperance, Ord River, Mt Tom Price, Mt Newman, Ord River, Kimberley and Hamersley ranges, Broome, surfing, fishing, sailing, wildflowers.

> **DID YOU KNOW?**
> Western Australia is three and a half times as big as Texas.

Western Australian flag

Western Australian coat of arms

Flag

The flag of Western Australia is based on the Blue Ensign, with the badge of the state superimposed on the right-hand side. It has a black swan within a yellow circle. This badge was granted in 1875.

Coat of arms

The present coat of arms was granted by Queen Elizabeth II in 1969. It incorporates a shield depicting a black swan, the bird emblem of the state. It is supported by two kangaroos, each holding a boomerang. The crest features an Imperial Crown surrounded by branches of kangaroo-paw, the state's floral emblem.

Perth, City of Lights

Major festivals

January	Perth Hyde Park Festival
	Mandurah Kanyana Festival
February	Festival of Perth
March	Albany Mardi Gras
	Swan River Festival
	Perth Swan Valley Wine Festival
August	Derby Boat Festival
	Exmouth Gala Festival
	Karratha–Dampier Fenacl Festival
	Newman Fortescue Festival
	Geraldton Sunshine Festival
	Tom Price (nameless) festival
	Kununurra–Ord Festival
	Paraburdoo Paragala Festival
	Broome Shinju Matsuri Festival
	Wyndham Top of the West Festival
	Carnarvon Tropical Festival
September	Perth Italian Spring Festival
October	Perth Oktoberfest
November	Fremantle Week
December	Perth–Australian Latvian Arts Festival

Sister cities

Albany	Kessennuma (Japan)
Broome	Taichi-Cho (Japan)
Fremantle	Yokosuka (Japan)
Perth	Kagoshima (Japan)
	Houston (Texas, USA)
	Rhodes (Greece)
	Island of Megisti (Greece)

DID YOU KNOW?
Wolf Creek, Western Australia, has the largest meteorite crater in Australia, 853.44 metres in diameter and 61 metres deep.

Tasmania

State capital
Hobart, the second oldest city in Australia, is situated on the Derwent River on the Tasman Peninsula. It has an area of 936 square kilometres and a population of 178 100. Average daily hours of sunshine, 5.8.

Largest cities
Hobart (178 100)
Launceston (89 740)
Burnie and Devonport (76 390)

Tasmanian floral emblem: southern blue gum

Location
The island state lies 240 kilometres off the south-eastern corner of the Australian continent, and is separated from the mainland by Bass Strait.

Area
It is the smallest state in Australia with an area of 67 800 square kilometres.

Landform
Mountainous, with lakes, cascades and steeply falling rivers.

Population
446 900, mostly on the north and east coasts.

Climate
Generally temperate, but the temperature often falls below 0ºC. There is high rainfall with very cold winters and cool summers.

Tasmania—gross value of production

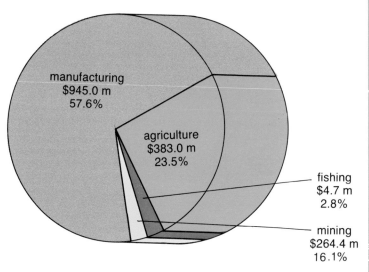

manufacturing
$945.0 m
57.6%

agriculture
$383.0 m
23.5%

fishing
$4.7 m
2.8%

mining
$264.4 m
16.1%

Chief products

Agricultural:

Timber, beef, canned fruit, dairy products, hops, mutton, potatoes, wool, lavender.

Fishing:

Barracouta, crayfish, salmon, scallops.

Manufacturing:

Aluminium, alginate, frozen food, pulp, paper.

Mining:

Coal, copper, gold, iron, lead, zinc, tin.

Main attractions

Snowfields, unspoiled mountain landscapes, historical places, Launceston and Hobart casinos, national parks, fishing, Franklin River, magnificent seascapes, thermal pools, Tasmanian devil, Gordon River. Tasmania is known as 'The Holiday Isle' and tourism is an important industry.

DID YOU KNOW?
Port Arthur, Tasmania, has ruins of prison cells four storeys high.

Tasmanian flag

Tasmanian coat of arms

Flag

The flag of Tasmania is based on the Blue Ensign with the badge of the state superimposed on the right-hand side. It consists of a red lion in a white circle. This badge was chosen in 1876.

Coat of arms

The present coat of arms was granted by King George V in 1917. It incorporates a shield on which is depicted a ram, a sheaf of wheat and apples, representing the pastoral and agricultural industries. Also included is a thunderbolt, which represents the hydro-electric schemes. The crest consists of a red lion standing with one paw resting on a spade and pickaxe which represents the mining industry. The shield is supported by two Tasmanian tigers. These are standing on ornamental supports above the motto *Ubertas et fidelitas* (Productiveness and faithfulness).

DID YOU KNOW?

Cradle Mountain Lake St Clair, Tasmania, is 134 804.66 hectares in size and is Australia's largest national park.

Major festivals

January	Sydney to Hobart Yacht Race (arrival)
	Devonport to Melbourne Yacht Race
	Huon Open Market
March	Launceston Batman Festival
	Devonport Mersey Valley Festival of Music
April	State-wide National Heritage Week
September	Stanley Circular Head Arts Festival
October	Devonport Rhododendron Festival
November	Deloraine Tasmania Cottage Industry Exhibition and Trade Fair
December	Hobart Salamanca Arts Festival

Sister cities

Hobart	Yaizu (Japan)
Launceston	Ikeda (Japan)

Port Arthur

Northern Territory

Location

The Northern Territory occupies a huge area of the continent's north and centre. It is bordered by the Timor Sea to the north, Queensland to the east, Western Australia to the west and South Australia to the south. Usually known as 'Outback Australia'.

Area

The Northern Territory comprises one-sixth of Australia's land mass and is 1 346 200 square kilometres in area.

Landform

Mostly desert and tablelands.

Population

148 100. Few people live in the the huge dry areas, and half the population are residents of Darwin. More than one-quarter of the people are Aboriginals.

Climate

The Northern Territory lies in the torrid zone. There are two broad climatic divisions—the northern part, known as 'The Top End' receives heavy rainfall for three to five months of the year, and the southern area, known as 'The Centre', has a low rainfall and no permanent rivers.

Administrative centre

Darwin is situated at Beagle Gulf on the Timor Sea and is 11 660 square kilometres in area. It has a population of 68 500. Average daily hours of sunshine, 8.5.

Chief towns

Darwin (68 500)
Alice Springs (23 300)
Katherine (4600)
Nhulunbuy (3900)
Tennant Creek (3200)

Northern Territory animal emblem: red kangaroo

Northern Territory floral emblem: Sturt's desert rose

Northern Territory—gross value of production

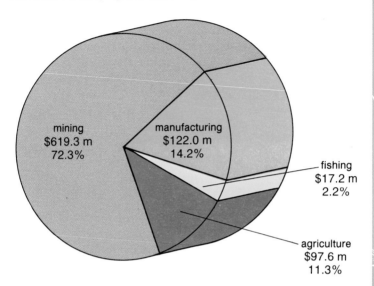

mining
$619.3 m
72.3%

manufacturing
$122.0 m
14.2%

fishing
$17.2 m
2.2%

agriculture
$97.6 m
11.3%

Chief products

Agricultural:

Beef cattle, citrus fruits, tomatoes, lucerne, peanuts, pineapples, timber.

Fishing:

Prawns and fish.

Mining:

Aluminium, bauxite, copper, iron, gold, manganese, tin, uranium.

Main attractions

Mt Olga National Park, Kings Canyon, Standley Chasm, The Ghan (the train from Adelaide to Alice Springs), Katherine Gorge, Bathurst and Melville islands, Kakadu National Park, Uluru National Park (Ayers Rock)

DID YOU KNOW?
Ayers Rock is a red granite monolith, 859.53 metres above sea level. It is 8.85 kilometres in circumference, and is 347.3 metres above the plain.

Northern Territory flag

Flag

The flag of the Northern Territory is very different from the other states' flags. Traditional Territory colours are used: black, white, and red ochre. The stars on the black panel represent the Southern Cross. On the red ochre panel appears Sturt's desert rose. This flag was proclaimed in 1978.

Northern Territory coat of arms

Coat of arms

The present coat of arms was granted by Queen Elizabeth II in 1978. It incorporates a shield depicting an Arnhem Land rock painting of an Aboriginal woman. On either side there are stylised journey or path markings of the Aboriginals. The shield is supported by two red kangaroos. In the fore-paw of one is a true heart cockle and in the fore-paw of the other is a spider conch. This all rests on a grassy mound from which grow Sturt's desert roses. The crest consists of a wedge-tailed eagle with wings splayed and its talons grasping an Aboriginal ritual stone or *Tjurunga*.

DID YOU KNOW?

Lake Eyre, 16 metres below sea level, is the lowest elevation. It is the driest area, receiving only 8–12 mm annual rainfall. Alice Springs is 609.6 metres above sea level.

Major festivals

January	Katherine Australia Day Bush Picnic
May	Tennant Creek Lions' Gold Rush Festival
	Alice Springs Bangtail Muster
	Alice Springs Lions' Camel Cup Carnival
June	Katherine Carnival
	Darwin Beer Can Regatta
August	Mataranka Bushman's Carnival
	Tennant Creek Folk Festival
	Alice Springs Henley-on-Todd Regatta

Sister cities

Darwin	Anchorage (Alaska, USA)
	Kalymnos (Greece)

Devils Marbles

People and performances

Prime ministers

Sir Edmund Barton (1 Jan 1901–24 Sept 1903)

Alfred Deakin (24 Sept 1903–27 Apr 1904)

John Christian Watson (27 Apr 1904–18 Aug 1904)

George Reid (18 Aug 1904–5 July 1905)

Alfred Deakin (5 July 1905–13 Nov 1908)

Andrew Fisher (13 Nov 1908–2 June 1909)

Alfred Deakin (2 June 1909–29 Apr 1910)

Andrew Fisher (29 Apr 1910–24 June 1913)

Sir Joseph Cook (24 June 1913–17 Sept 1914)

Andrew Fisher (17 Sept 1914–27 Oct 1915)

William Morris Hughes (27 Oct 1915–9 Feb 1922)

Stanley Melbourne Bruce (9 Feb 1922–22 Oct 1929)

James Henry Scullin (22 Oct 1929–6 Jan 1932)

Joseph Aloysius Lyons
(6 Jan 1932–7 Apr 1939)

Sir Earle Page (7 Apr 1939–
26 Apr 1939)

Sir Robert Gordon Menzies
(26 Apr 1939–29 Aug 1941)

Sir Arthur W Fadden (29 Aug
1941–7 Oct 1941)

John Curtin (7 Oct 1941–
5 July 1945)

Francis Michael Forde (6 July
1945–13 July 1945)

Joseph Benedict Chifley
(13 July 1945–19 Dec 1949)

Sir Robert Gordon Menzies
(19 Dec 1949–26 Jan 1966)

Harold Edward Holt
(26 Jan 1966–19 Dec 1967)

Sir John McEwen (19 Dec
1967–10 Jan 1968)

Sir John Grey Gorton
(10 Jan 1968–10 Mar 1971)

Sir William McMahon (10 Mar
1971–8 Dec 1972)

Edward Gough Whitlam
(8 Dec 1972–11 Nov 1975)

John Malcolm Fraser (11 Nov
1975–5 Mar 1983) (caretaker
prime minister from
11 Nov–13 Dec 1975)

Robert James Lee Hawke
(5 Mar 1983–)

Architecture

Edmund Blackett 1817–83

An early colonial architect
who designed churches.

Robin Boyd 1919–71

He was a writer as well as an
architect. An influential critic
of Australian aesthetics, he
published *The Australian
Ugliness* in 1960.

Francis Greenway 1777–1837

In 1816 Greenway, a convict,
became the colony's official
architect, under the guidance
of Governor Macquarie.

Sir Roy Grounds 1905–81

Exponent of the new
'international' style of
architecture of the 1950s. He
is best known for his
Academy of Sciences
building in Canberra and the
Victorian Arts Centre in
Melbourne.

Harry Seidler 1923–

Contemporary Australian
architect. Designed Australia
Square Tower and the MLC
Building in Sydney, the Hong
Kong Club and the Australian
embassy in Paris.

DID YOU KNOW?
Sydney Tower, at Centrepoint, is the highest building in
the southern hemisphere, 324.8 metres above sea level.

Victorian Arts Centre

Science

Sir Macfarlane Burnet 1899–1985

Researcher and biologist. Winner of Nobel Prize for medicine, noted for his research into control of disease, particularly poliomyelitis.

Professor Graeme Clarke 1935–

A researcher and professor of Otolaryngology at Melbourne University. In the late 1970s he was responsible for the development of the bionic ear which is a cochlea implant designed to provide electrical stimulation to the inner ear to overcome the effect of profound deafness.

Sir Ian Clunies-Ross 1899–1959

A scientist and administrator.

The first director of the Commonwealth Scientific Industrial Research Organisation, a statutory body, created to carry out scientific research relevant to the national and international interests of Australia.

Sir John Eccles 1903–

A scientist who contributed greatly to the knowledge of the way nerves interact with the spinal cord.

Lord (Howard) Florey 1898–1968

Scientist and Nobel Prize winner for medicine. Pioneered penicillin treatment.

Dr Priscilla Kincaid-Smith 1926–

The director of nephrology at Royal Melbourne Hospital. In 1968 she was the first person to link long-term dosing with analgesics to renal disease.

Dr William Griffith McBride 1927–

A doctor who alerted the world to the dangers of taking Thalidomide during pregnancy (1961).

Sir Marcus Oliphant 1901–

Nuclear physicist and first president of Australian Academy of Science. Assistant director of research with Rutherford at the Cavendish Laboratory in

Cambridge in 1935. Now consistently opposed to nuclear weapons.

Aviation

Sir Reginald Ansett 1909–1981

A businessman and outspoken champion of private enterprise. His companies were involved in aviation, transport, tourism and television.

John Duigan 1882–1951

In 1910 he constructed the first Australian-built aeroplane to fly.

Sir Hudson Fysh 1895–1974

Together with P J McGinness he founded the airline Queensland and Northern Territory Air Services (QANTAS) in 1920.

Lawrence Hargrave 1850–1915 and George A Taylor 1872–1928

In the 1890s these two men experimented with box kites. Taylor in 1909 achieved a flight of 100 metres at Narrabeen Heads, New South Wales.

Harry George Hawker 1889–1921

Hawker became internationally famous in 1913 for the most successful attempt to circumnavigate the British Isles in 72 hours.

Bert Hinkler 1892–1933

Known as 'The Lone Eagle', in 1928 he flew the longest solo flight from London to Darwin, in a record 16 days.

Amy Johnson 1903–41

She was the first woman to fly from England to Australia. Her 1930 epic solo flight, in a D H Moth, took 19 days.

Sir Charles Kingsford Smith 1897–1935

Pioneer aviator. In 1928, flying the famous monoplane *Southern Cross*, he, Charles Ulm (1897–1934) and two Americans were the first men to fly across the Pacific. This venture included one of the longest non-stop flights ever attempted between Honolulu and Fiji (35 hours). Total flying time 83 hours 38 minutes.

DID YOU KNOW?
Sydney's Opera House was designed by Danish architect Jörn Utzon in 1957. Construction began in 1959 and it was officially opened by Queen Elizabeth II in 1973.

Keith Smith 1890–1955 and Ross Smith 1892–1922

These men pioneered the London to Sydney air route in 1919, taking 27 days 27 minutes. Their total flying time for the 18 500 kilometres was 135 hours 50 minutes.

Engineering and inventions

Sir John (Jack) Brabham 1926–

Racing-car driver. He went from winning the 1948 Australian Speedway Championship in a home-made car, to winning three World Grand Prix.

John Bradfield 1867–1943

He designed the Sydney Harbour Bridge which was begun in 1923 and completed in 1931, at a cost of 9 577 507 pounds (equivalent to $127 million in 1985).

Sir Ernest Fisk 1886–1965

Pioneered radio in Australia. In 1918 he picked up the first direct wireless message from England at his home in Sydney.

Sir Edward Hallstrom 1886–1970

An inventor who helped develop refrigeration in Australia. He flew with inventor-aviator George A Taylor in 1909.

Sir William Hudson 1896–1978

Commissioner in charge of the Snowy Mountains Hydro-Electric Scheme which diverts the waters of the Snowy and Eucumbene rivers through two tunnel systems, westwards under the Great Dividing Range, to feed two inland rivers, the Murray and Murrumbidgee. The scheme provides water for irrigation and also produces electricity from seven power stations for NSW, Victoria, and the ACT.

Essington Lewis 1881–1961

Industrialist responsible for the Broken Hill Proprietary Company shifting its emphasis from mining to steel. BHP is Australia's largest company.

DID YOU KNOW?

Rupert Murdoch, the newspaper magnate, has been listed as Australia's wealthiest person. (In 1985 Murdoch took out US citizenship.) Next come J and R Ingham, Kerry Packer, Robert Holmes a Court, John Kahlbetzer, and the Smorgon and Reid families.

Evelyn Ernest Owen 1915–49

In the 1930s he invented the revolutionary Owen sub-machine gun.

Ralph Sarich 1938–

An inventor with many innovative projects to his credit. These are in the field of fuel injection and irrigation systems. He is more widely known for his research in the development of the orbital combustion process engine and attached technologies.

Business

Lawrence (Larry) Adler 1931–

A successful businessman who has been the chairman of F.A.I. Insurance Group since 1960.

Alan Bond 1938–

An entrepreneur and businessman who began his career as a signwriter. He is the chairman of the Bond Corporation Holdings Limited. Headed the Australian syndicate which won the America's Cup.

Sir Warwick Fairfax 1901–1987

Former chairman of John Fairfax Ltd. with interests in newspapers, magazines, television and radio. His influence on the editorial policy of the *Sydney Morning Herald* had a great impact on Australian society.

Lang Hancock 1909–

Discovered massive iron-ore deposits on the Pilbara, WA, where he began the Australian iron-ore mining industry, 1952–62.

Robert Holmes a Court 1937–

Chairman of Associated Communication Corporation and The Bell Group Ltd Australia.

Kerry Packer 1937–

He is chairman and managing director of Consolidated Press Holdings, Publishing and Broadcasting Ltd and director general of Television Corporation Ltd. He played a major role in popularising one-day cricket matches.

Cartoonists

J C Banks 1880–1952

Created the much-loved character Ginger Meggs.

Frank Benier c 1923–

A highly talented, traditional cartoonist whose humour has spanned several decades. His cartoons of Henry Bolte, the premier of Victoria 1955–72, are legendary.

Eric Jolliffe c 1907–

A post-war comic artist whose series *Witchetty's Tribe*, with its contrasts of Aboriginal and Western values, has been popular for decades.

Lennie Lower 1903–47

He was a prolific newspaper columnist of the 1930s and 1940s and one of Australia's greatest humorists. *Here's Another*, published in 1932, was a collection of humorous sketches.

Emile Mercier c 1909–81

A vigorous comic artist of the 1950s and 1960s, whose zany humour is forever remembered for its incidental details, particularly about gravy cans.

Syd Nicholls 1897–1977

His cartoon character, Fatty Finn, was second only to Ginger Meggs in popularity and longevity.

Bruce Petty 1929–

He is widely regarded as one of the world's finest political cartoonists and as the most committed and intellectual of contemporary Australian cartoonists. His cartoons began to appear in the *Australian* in 1965.

Ron Tandberg 1943–

A political cartoonist with the Melbourne *Age*. His simple line drawings make terse comments on current news stories.

Literature

Thea Astley 1925–

A novelist who is a three-time winner of the Miles Franklin Award. She published *A Descant for Gossips* in 1960, and *An Item from the Late News* in 1982.

Alexander Buzo 1944–

Satirist of Australian manners and morals. He wrote *The Revolt*, 1967, and *Norm and Ahmed*, 1968.

Eleanor Dark 1901–85

Author of historical novels of early Australia, *The Timeless Land*, 1941, and *Storm of Time*, 1948.

Bruce Dawe 1930–

Poet and novelist. His works include *No Fixed Address*, 1962, and *Condolences of the Season*, 1971.

C J Dennis 1876–1938

A journalist and poet. He was known as 'The Laureate of the Larrikin' because he wrote a series of verse stories told in slang. One of these was the best-selling Australian book of the First World War, *The Song of the Sentimental Bloke*.

M Barnard Eldershaw

This was the pen-name of a very successful literary collaboration between

Marjory F Barnard, 1897– , a short-story writer, and Flora Eldershaw, 1897–1956, a teacher. Among their works was *A House is Built*, 1929.

Alec Derwent Hope 1907–

A poet who has published many volumes of poetry including *The Wandering Islands*, 1955, and *The Drifting Continent*, 1979.

Miles Franklin 1879–1954

A novelist. She wrote the satirical novel, *My Brilliant Career*, about 1899 (published 1901).

Dame Mary Gilmore 1865–1962

A poet, writer and social worker who championed the underdog. Her book of verse, *Under the Wilgas*, was published in 1932.

Germaine Greer 1939–

Feminist and author of *The Female Eunuch*, 1970, and *Sex and Destiny*, 1984.

Frank Hardy 1917–

Novelist and writer of short stories. His *Power Without Glory*, 1950, led to a libel suit against him. It was not successful.

Max Harris 1921–

A poet, critic and journalist. He was the central figure in the modern verse movement in Adelaide in the 1940s. He published the *Angry Penguins* journal from 1941 to 1964.

Shirley Hazzard 1931–

An expatriate novelist and short-story writer who has had works published in the *New Yorker*. Her novels include *The Transit of Venus*, 1980. *Cliffs of Fall*, 1963, is a collection of short stories.

Xavier Herbert 1901–84

A novelist. *Capricornia*, one of the classics of Australian literature, was written in 1938. His later work, *Poor Fellow My Country*, 1975, is also highly regarded.

Donald Horne 1921–

A political and social commentator, he wrote *A Lucky Country* in 1967, and *The Story of the Australian People*, 1972.

David Ireland 1927–

He is one of Australia's foremost novelists. His published works include the play *Image in Clay*, 1964, and the novels *The Unknown Industrial Prisoner*, 1971, *The Glass Canoe*, 1976, and *A Woman of the Future*, 1979.

Clive James 1939–

Born in Australia, he is known as an author and television critic in England. He wrote *Visions Before Midnight*, *Unreliable Memoirs*, 1980, and *Flying Visits*, 1985.

George Johnston 1912–70

A novelist, he wrote the semi-autobiographical novel *My Brother Jack*, 1964.

Nancy Keesing, 1923–

Poet and author. Her works include *Lily on the Dustbin*, 1982, and *Shalom*, 1983.

Thomas Keneally 1935–

A novelist he won the Miles Franklin Award in 1967 for his book *Bring Larks and Heroes*. He also wrote *The Chant of Jimmie Blacksmith,* 1972, and *Schindler's Ark*, 1982, which won him the Booker Prize in Great Britain.

Ray Lawler 1922–

Playwright and actor. His play *The Summer of the Seventeenth Doll*, which broke new ground in Australian theatre, was first produced in 1955.

Henry Lawson 1867–1922

Author and poet. He became popular with his ballad-type verses and short stories. Most famous are the selection of poems *In the Days when the World was Wide*, 1896 (see Chapter 8), and the short-story collection *Joe Wilson and his Mates*, 1901.

David Malouf 1934–

A poet and novelist. His books include *Bicycles*, 1970, *Johnno*, 1976, *First Things Last* and *An Imaginary Life*, 1980, and *Fly Away Peter*, 1983.

Les Murray 1938–

A highly regarded poet. His books include three volumes of selected poems, *The Vernacular Republic*, 1976, *Ethnic Radio*, 1978, and *People's Otherworld*, 1983.

A B ('Banjo') Paterson 1864–1941

Poet and journalist. He captured the atmosphere of the bush with racing, evocative rhythms. His most famous poem is 'The Man from Snowy River', 1892 (see Chapter 8).

Hal Porter 1911–84

Playwright and author. His books include *Watcher on the Cast Iron Balcony*, 1963, and *The Extra*, 1975.

Katharine Susannah Prichard 1884–1969

She wrote novels with Australian themes and strong overtones of social protest. *Coonardoo* was published in 1929.

DID YOU KNOW?
Hobart is the home of Australia's oldest surviving theatre—The Royal in Campbell Street.

Henry Handel Richardson 1870–1946

A novelist, her real name was Ethel Richardson. Her masterpiece, *The Fortunes of Richard Mahony*, was written during 1917–29 and published in 1929.

Steele Rudd (Arthur Hoey Davis) 1868–1935

He wrote humorous novels of life on a small selection (farm), and created the characters Dad and Dave. *On Our Selection* was first published in 1899.

Kenneth Slessor 1901–71

Considered one of Australia's finest poets. His writings, and in particular his war poems, are powerful and stimulating. His poems include 'Five Bells', 1939, and 'Beach Burial', 1942.

Christina Stead 1902–1984

An author who first gained fame overseas. Her best known works are *Seven Poor Men of Sydney*, 1934, and *The Man Who Loved Children*, 1940.

Douglas Stewart 1913–1985

Born in New Zealand, he was a journalist, poet and literary critic, who for thirty years influenced Australian literature. His works include the plays *Fire on the Snow*, 1941, and *Ned Kelly*, 1943.

Randolph Stow 1935–

Poet and novelist. His works include *To The Islands*, 1958, and *The Merry-go-round in the Sea*, 1965.

Kath Walker 1920–

An Aboriginal poet who expresses her feelings powerfully and with passion. Her poetry collections include *My People*, 1970, *Father Sky and Mother Earth*, 1981, and *Stradbroke Dreamtime*, 1982.

Morris West 1916–

He deliberately sought experiences to enrich his writing. His internationally known novels include *Children of the Sun*, 1957, and *The Shoes of the Fisherman*, 1963.

Patrick White 1912–

Considered to be Australia's greatest novelist, he was the first Australian to be awarded the Nobel Prize for literature. He published *Tree of Man* in 1955, *Voss* in 1957, *The Vivisector* in 1970, and *A Fringe of Leaves*, 1976. In recent years he has concentrated on writing plays such as *Signal Driver*, 1984.

David Williamson 1942–

Internationally acclaimed playwright. His works include *The Removalists*, 1971, *Jugglers Three*, 1972, *The Department*, 1975, and *What if You Died Tomorrow?*, 1985, *Emerald City*, 1986.

Judith Wright 1915–

A leading poet and author. Her books include *Woman to Man*, 1949, *Collected Poems*, 1971, and *Cry for the Dead*, 1981.

Stage, screen and radio

Dame Judith Anderson 1898–

An Adelaide actress of world fame. She won the Donaldson Award for most distinguished actress in the American theatre, 1948.

Oscar Asche 1871–1936

Actor and playwright. Author of the Orient-inspired musical, *Chu Chin Chow*, 1916.

Bert Bailey 1872–1953

Actor, famous for the part of Dad in *On Our Selection*, 1931, a feature film comedy based on Steele Rudd's characters.

Tony Barber 1940–

A television compere and host of Network Nine's top rating quiz show, 'Sale of the Century'. He began his career in television as the 'Cambridge Whistler' in a cigarette commercial in 1969.

Bryan Brown 1948–

An actor of international fame, noted for his roles in the film *Breaker Morant*, 1979, and the television series *A Town Like Alice*, 1980.

Tom Burlinson 1956–

Actor in television and films. He starred in the films *The Man from Snowy River*, 1983, and *Phar Lap*, 1983.

Ita Buttrose 1942–

A journalist, broadcaster and television personality. In 1972 she designed and launched a magazine called *Cleo*, and was appointed editor of the Australian *Women's Weekly* in 1975. Recently she has been involved with radio and television programmes and in 1985 she became chairwoman of the National Advisory Committee on AIDS (Acquired-Immune Deficiency Syndrome).

Gordon Chater 1922–

An English-born actor well known in Australia for his role in the television series 'My Name's McGooley'. He became renowned in the United States for his role in the Australian play, *The Elocution of Benjamin Franklin*, in 1984.

DID YOU KNOW?
The first television station in Australia opened in 1956 as TCN Channel 9, Sydney.

Diane Cilento 1932–

An actress of stage and film. Her performance on Broadway in *Tiger at the Gates* won her the Critics' Choice Award as best actress of the year, 1955.

Jack Davey 1910–59

A popular radio personality of the 1940s and 1950s. His famous greeting was 'Hi ho everybody!'.

Judy Davis 1955–

An actress of stage and screen, she played a starring role in the film *My Brilliant Career*, 1978, Golda in the British film of that name, 1981, and Adela in *A Passage to India*, 1984.

Bob Dyer 1907–84

Radio and television personality. With his wife Dolly, he set a record for the longest-running television show, 'Pick A Box', which was produced for a period of fourteen years from 1957 to 1971. His 'Howdy customers', 'Tell them Bob sent you' and 'The money or the box' were household sayings.

Peter Finch 1915–77

A film and theatre actor of West End fame. He appeared in Chauvel's *The Rats of Tobruk*, 1949.

Dame Doris Fitton 1897–

An actress and theatre director, she opened the Sydney Independent Theatre Company in 1930.

Errol Flynn 1909–59

A swashbuckling, Hobart-born actor, notorious on and off the screen. He was most famous for his title role in the film *Captain Blood*, 1935.

Mel Gibson 1956–

An actor, he has had starring roles in *Mad Max I*, 1979, *II*, 1982, and *Mad Max: Beyond Thunderdome,* 1985, *The Year of Living Dangerously,* 1983, and *Mrs Soffel*, 1985.

John Hargreaves 1946–

An actor of stage and screen, he played lead roles in the films *The Removalists*, 1975, *Don's Party*, 1976, and *Careful, He Might Hear You*, 1983.

Dorothy Helmrich 1889–1984

She was the first Australian to achieve world-wide recognition as a lieder singer. She founded the Arts Council movement in Australia in 1943 to enable the youth of the nation to experience music and the arts.

Derryn Hinch 1944–

A journalist and broadcaster who is presently a current affairs presenter for Channel 7 television, Melbourne. He won a gold award at the International Radio Festival in New York in 1983 for his live broadcast from China to Melbourne. A controversial figure who is noted for his forthright approach to situations.

Paul Hogan ('Hoges') 1940–

A comic entertainer. His 'Crocodile Dundee' character enjoys wide popularity at home and overseas.

Wendy Hughes 1950–

A film actress, internationally acclaimed for her performances in *Newsfront*, 1978, and *Careful, He Might Hear You*, 1983.

Barry Humphries 1934–

A satirist, author and actor, he created the characters of Dame Edna Everage and Les Patterson.

Graham Kennedy 1934–

Television compere and actor. In 1957 he became compere of the variety show, 'In Melbourne Tonight', which ran until 1970.

John Laws 1935–

He began his career in country radio in Victoria in 1955 and became a versatile broadcaster journalist, actor, poet and singer. He is presently working with the Macquarie network in Sydney.

Mark Lee 1957–

An actor and rock musician. He played a starring role in the film *Gallipoli*, 1982.

John Meillon 1934–

An acclaimed actor of stage and film, he was noted for his performance of the father in the film *The Fourth Wish*, 1976.

Ian ('Molly') Meldrum 1945–

A television talent co-ordinator, he is one of the most influential figures in the Australian rock-music scene. He was with the ABC show 'Countdown' from 1975 until 1987.

Bert Newton 1938–

A winner of thirteen Logies, Bert, with his twin talents as a natural comedian and sophisticated compere, has been a favourite with visiting celebrities, viewers and critics alike. He began his career in the late 1950s and he is still a popular personality.

DID YOU KNOW?
The oldest daily newspaper in the southern hemisphere is the *Sydney Morning Herald* (1831).

Trisha (Patsy-Anne) Noble 1945–

A vocalist and actress now living in the United States. She has appeared often as a guest star in Hollywood films and American television series. She began her career with the television show 'Bandstand' in the late 1960s.

Jill Perryman 1933–

A musical-comedy star who came to fame in J C Williamson's production of *Call Me Madam*, 1953. She played the dramatic role of Jessie in the play *Night Mother* with June Salter, 1984.

Nat Phillips 1883–1932 and Roy Rene 1892–1954 ('Stiffy' and 'Mo')

A vaudeville team from the 1920s to 1930s, they delighted and scandalised audiences with their bawdy humour. Many of Mo's sayings are still quoted: 'Strike me lucky' and 'You little trimmer'.

Chips Rafferty 1909–71

An actor and producer, he was famous for his portrayal of the typical Australian bushman. He appeared in Chauvel's *The Rats of Tobruk*, 1949.

Jack Thompson 1941–

A popular actor of stage and film. He appeared in the films *Sunday Too Far Away*, 1975, *Breaker Morant*, 1979, and *The Man From Snowy River*, 1983.

George Wallace 1894–1960

A comedian. His most famous film was *Gone to the Dogs*, c 1930.

Mike Walsh 1938–

A television producer, talk-show host and interviewer, he is one of Australia's most popular personalities of television. He went from being a country radio announcer in 1960 to hosting one of the most popular daytime shows of Australian television. The daytime 'Mike Walsh Show' ran from 1973 to 1984.

John Waters 1945–

An actor of stage and screen, he performed in the television series 'Rush', and in the plays *They're Playing Our Song*, 1980, and *Children of a Lesser God*, 1984.

Jackie Weaver 1947–

An actress of both film and stage. She starred in the musical comedy *They're Playing Our Song*, 1980, and the stage play *Born Yesterday*, 1984.

Peter Weir 1944–

Film director who has many box office hits to his credit, including *Picnic at Hanging Rock*, 1975; *The Last Wave*,

1977; *Gallipoli*, 1981; *The Year of Living Dangerously*, 1982 and more recently has been successful in Hollywood with the films *Witness*, 1985, which had academy award nominations, and *The Mosquito Coast*, 1986.

Mike Willesee 1942–

A journalist and television compere. At 22, he was the youngest ever fully accredited political correspondent in Canberra. He has compered many television current affairs programmes and in 1984 joined the Nine Network with the 'Willesee' public affairs programme and documentary series.

J C Williamson 1835–1913

Theatrical entrepreneur and founder of the theatrical company of the same name, which is still one of the largest companies of its type in the world.

Music

Don Banks 1923–80

A leading Australian composer specialising in composition of electronic music. His early composition *Four Pieces for orchestra*, was performed by the London Philharmonic Orchestra in 1954.

Richard Bonynge 1930–

An opera conductor and the musical director of The Australian Opera since 1976. His official conducting debut was in 1962 with the Santa Cecilia Orchestra in Rome. He has many recordings and performances to his credit and is renowned for his interest in the lesser-known operas of the 17th and 18th centuries. He is married to Joan Sutherland.

June Bronhill, 1931–

Soprano of opera and musical comedy. She changed her surname to honour Broken Hill, the town where she was born which had encouraged her wonderful talent. She won the Sun Aria competition in 1950 and from then on her success was assured.

John Brownlee 1901–69

A world-famous operatic baritone who was encouraged by Dame Nellie Melba. He sang duets with her in the early 1900s, in productions by famous overseas opera companies.

DID YOU KNOW?
The first radio station in Australia was built near Pennant Hills, Sydney, in 1912.

Don Burrows 1928–

With a career spanning more than thirty years, he is one of Australia's most distinguished jazz musicians (flute and clarinet). His performance at Carnegie Hall at the New York Jazz Festival in 1972 was well received. He is renowned for his interest in children's music.

Nigel Butterley 1935–

A composer of contemporary music who specialises in music for string quartets. He was awarded the prestigious Italia Prize for *In the Head the Fire*, commissioned by the Australian Broadcasting Commission (ABC). In recent years his music has been inspired by the poetry of Walt Whitman.

Peter Dawson 1892–1961

A world-renowned bass baritone, his recording career extended from wax cylinders to tape. His best-selling record was 'Floral Dance', 1926.

Percy Grainger 1882–1961

A pianist and composer of international fame. As a child he gave concerts throughout Australia and at the age of eleven he began his studies in Germany. His uninhibited irreverent approach to the piano delighted audiences everywhere. His most famous compositions were

Joan Sutherland in The Merry Widow, *1979*

Shepherd's Hey and *Country Garden,* c 1907.

Joan Hammond 1912–

A soprano, she was an operatic star of the 1930s and 1940s. She sang one of the Valkyries in the Fuller's Royal Grand Opera presentation of *Die Walküre*.

Eileen Joyce 1912–

An international concert pianist. In the 1950s she had the widest following of any concert pianist in England.

Dame Nellie Melba 1861–1931

A world-acclaimed lyric soprano, she toured extensively in Britain, on the Continent and in the United States. Gounod coached her in the role of Juliet in his opera *Romeo and Juliet*. She was also chosen by Puccini to play Mimi in his opera, *La Bohème*, c 1900. She was revered as the supreme soprano of her time.

Gladys Moncrieff 1892–1976

Known as 'Our Glad', she was a popular soprano, noted for her portrayal of Teresa in *Maid of the Mountains*, for which she received eighteen curtain calls during a performance in 1921. She starred at The Gaiety and Daly's theatres in London with great success, returning to Australia to enthusiastic audiences.

Peter Sculthorpe 1929–

One of Australia's foremost and talented contemporary composers. From 1965 to 1967 he wrote *Sun Music I II III IV* based on the Australian landscape. In 1974 the Australian Opera produced his full-length opera *Rites of Passage* and in 1982 the ABC televised his opera *Quiros*.

Dame Joan Sutherland 1926–

A brilliant coloratura soprano of international acclaim, she made the first of many appearances with the Royal Opera Company at Covent Garden in the role of First Lady in Mozart's *Die Zauberflöte*. Her international status was established when the Royal Opera Company presented her in Donizetti's *Lucia di Lammermoor* in 1959. She is married to Richard Bonynge.

John Williams 1941–

One of the world's leading classical guitarists displaying in his music strong economical technique and clear quality of tone. At the age of twelve he studied with the famous Andres Segovia, after which he toured extensively. In 1979 he formed the jazz-oriented group Sky which has enjoyed wide success.

Malcolm Williamson 1931–

A prolific composer, he was appointed Master of the Queen's Music in 1975. His best-known work is the music for Sir Robert Helpmann's ballet, *The Display*, 1964. That same year his opera *English Eccentrics* was premiered at Aldeburgh Festival, England. He is particularly interested in music therapy for handicapped children.

Roger Woodward 1942–

An internationally renowned pianist. He extended his studies in London and Warsaw and made his debut with the Warsaw National Philharmonic Orchestra in 1967. He has a particularly wide repertoire ranging from Australian contemporary music to Beethoven and Chopin.

Pop music

AC DC

In 1975 they were Australia's loudest, fastest and most aggressive pub rock band. By 1980 they were one of the most popular hard rock bands in the world with such hits as 'High Voltage Rock 'n' Roll', 'Let there be Rock' and 'Highway to Hell' which gave them the reputation of having a very 'Aussie' sound.

Air Supply

Formed in 1976 and toured the United States with Rod Stewart. From 1980 to 1982 they had seven consecutive hits on five top international charts (which was more than the Beatles or Elvis Presley had). Their songs include 'Lost in Love', 'Every Woman in the World' and 'The One that you Love'.

Angels

With lead singer Doc Nesani, their athletic stage show attracted large audiences. Their hit songs included 'Shadow Boxer', 'Take a Long Line' and 'Stand Up'. When performing internationally they were known as Angel City.

Bee Gees

In the 1960s Barry, Robin and Maurice Gibb became a highly successful trio with many hit records. Their songs include 'New York Mining Disaster—1941', 1967, 'Massachusetts', 1967, 'I Started a Joke', 1969, and 'How Can You Mend a Broken Heart?', 1971. In 1977 their album 'Saturday Night Fever' was the score music for the film of the same name.

Eric Bogle 1944–

This Scottish-born folk singer has embraced the Aussie way of life and writes astute songs about Australian society. In

1972 he wrote 'And the Band Played Waltzing Matilda', and later 'Now I'm Easy' and 'I Hate Wogs'.

Bushwackers

A traditional bush-music band which has toured extensively here and overseas. The lead singer is Dove Newton and their record Marihuana Australiana was a hit in 1977.

Cobbers

A traditional bush-music band which specialises in day-to-day concerns. Their traditional arrangement of 'Waltzing Matilda' was well received, as was their 'Billy of Tea' and 'Spider by the Gwydir'.

Cold Chisel

One of Australia's top rock 'n' roll bands for more than a decade, they disbanded in late 1983. Some of their best-known hits were 'Cheap Wine', 'Shipping Steel' and 'Star Hotel'.

Daddy Cool

Under the leadership of guitarist and singer Ross Wilson, this band made a significant breakthrough for Australian music. The songs 'Come Back Again' and 'Eagle Rock' were their most successful singles.

Daly Wilson Big Band

They revived the big band sound and in 1977 toured extensively overseas and gained international fame, particularly in Russia. The band is now called the Warren Daly Big Band.

Delltones

This band first gained prominence when the surfing craze was at its height in the 1960s. Their song 'Hangin' Five' reflected the independent spirit of the times and assured them of continuing success.

Divinyls

They topped the Australian charts and then toured the United States with one-night stands. Their most popular songs are 'Only Lonely' and 'All the Boys in Town'.

Slim Dusty 1927–

He has dominated country and western music in Australia for over thirty years, and was the first Australian artist to make the international pop charts with 'Pub with no Beer' in 1959.

DID YOU KNOW?
The Australian coastline totals 36 735 kilometres.

Easy Beats

In 1966 they had five national hits in a row with strong, energetic songs like 'Friday On My Mind', and 'Wedding Ring'. They made the Top 10 on the British charts.

Jon English 1949–

A vocalist, actor and musical comedy star. He performed in the musicals *Hair*, *Jesus Christ Superstar* and *The Pirates of Penzance*, and has had the hit song 'Hot Town'.

John Farnham 1950–

First became popular as a solo artist with such singles as 'Sadie the Cleaning Lady', 1967, and 'Raindrops Keep Falling on My Head', 1968. In 1981, he became lead singer of the *Little River Band*. In 1986 produced the solo album, 'Whispering Jack'. Was voted King of Pop in 1987 by A.R.I.A.S.

Geisha

Formed in 1983, became well known with 'Rainy Day' and 'Kabuki', 1985, and 'Part Time Love Affair', 1986.

Goanna

Their hit song 'Solid Rock' protested against the destruction of Aboriginal culture.

Rolf Harris 1931–

He began his career in television in 1960. His song 'Tie Me Kangaroo Down, Sport', reached the top ten on the British charts.

Hunters and Collectors

During the 1980s they opened the eyes and ears of England and the United States with the musical diversity of their hit 'Talking to a Stranger'.

Ice House

A highly successful band, first in Germany then Canada and England. Their top hits were 'Hey Little Girl', and 'Great Southern Land'.

INXS

This band successfully played at the United States Music Festival in 1983 to an audience of over 300 000 people. Their song 'The One Thing' made the Top 40 in the United States.

Geisha

Mental as Anything

Men At Work

This was the first band to make number one on the United States charts with their first single and debut album. Their hit songs include 'Down Under' (which gained world-wide recognition as the celebratory song for Australia's victory in the America's Cup), 'Who Can it be Now', 'Overkill' and 'Be Good Johnny'.

Mental As Anything

This band formed for fun in 1980 and five years later were still successful. They gained international popularity with 'If You Leave Me Can I Come Too'.

Jo Jo Zep

In the 1980s they toured the United States and the Continent with their hit 'Taxi Mary', to great acclaim.

Midnight Oil

Primarily a politically motivated band. Songs such as 'Power and the Passion', 'US Forces' and 'A Place Without a Postcard' have given them a large following. Their lead singer is Peter Garrett.

Little River Band

They formed in 1974, with Glenn Shorrock as lead singer. Their recording, 'Help is on its Way', was popularised by radio in Jacksonville, Florida, and success was assured. By 1980 over 3 million of their albums were sold, making them the most successful group here and overseas. 'Take It Easy On Me' and 'Reminiscing' were some of their hits.

Models

A volatile band which has survived the transition from creative cult band to commercially viable pop group. 'Out of Mind, Out of Sight' was number one hit in Australia and it made the top 40 in the US. Other songs include 'Let's Kiss', 'Barbados', 'Evolution' and 'Hold On'.

Models

Pseudo Echo

This young group (22 is their average age) is dynamic, talented, fun loving and committed. Their album, 'Love An Adventure' and subsequent singles such as 'Don't Go' are much acclaimed.

Moving Pictures

A successful rock band here and in the United States with songs such as 'What About Me?', which hit the charts in 1982.

Olivia Newton-John 1950–

A popular Australian vocalist since 1965. In 1970 she made the world charts with the song, 'Banks of the Ohio'. Success came her way in the United States with her lead part in the musical *Grease*. In 1981 'Physical' became a smash hit and 'I Honestly Love You', co-written with Peter Allen, won her two Grammy Awards.

Johnny O'Keefe 1935–78

Known as the 'Boomerang Kid' or JO'K, he began his career in 1956 with the television show 'Six O'clock Rock'. He made the American charts with 'She's My Baby' written especially for him by rock 'n' roll king, Bill Haley.

Pseudo Echo

Helen Reddy 1941–

In 1965 she was the most successful vocalist in Australia. Her breakthrough came in the United States in 1972 with the single, 'I Am Woman', which became the theme song for the women's liberation movement.

Real Life

In 1983 they had their first Australian hit, 'Send me an

DID YOU KNOW?
The first rail service in Australia ran from Flinders Street to Port Melbourne in 1854. The Sydney–Parramatta rail service began in 1855.

133

Angel'. By 1984 they had rocketed up the Australian, German, Canadian and United States charts with 'Catch Me I'm Falling'.

Redgum

This is a socio-political folk band whose songs have overtones of sarcasm. 'I was Only Nineteen' was a massive hit in 1984 and the live album 'Caught in the Act' has sold over 100 000 copies in Australia. Their latest album is 'Midnight Sun'.

Rose Tattoo

This group, by relentless touring throughout the world, have achieved headline acceptance. 'Bad Boy For Love' and 'We Can't Be Beaten' are two of their hits.

The Seekers

A Melbourne folk group. From 1964 to 1968 Judith Durham, Keith Potger, Bruce Woodley and Athol Guy won international success. They topped the charts with 'Georgie Girl', but disbanded in 1968.

Sherbert

In 1976 their song 'Howzat' made it to the top of the charts here and in Britain.

Skyhooks

This group is recognised for its truly Australian flavour. Their songs are written by Greg Macainsh. 'Living in the 70s' was one of their most popular albums.

Rick Springfield 1950–

In 1970 he reached the top in Australia, with the band, Zoot. In 1972 his solo 'Speak to the Sky' made the charts in the United States. He had a breakthrough in 1980 with the song, 'Jessie's Girl'.

John Williamson 1945–

An observant lyricist and country folk singer whose songs reflect his deep sense of understanding human nature. His works include 'Old Man Emu' 1970 and 'Cootamundra Wattle' 1986, as well as 'True Blue' 1986 which became the catch cry for Australians to stop and think more about their country.

John Williamson

Uncanny X-Men

Beginning as a young garage band in late 1981, they have quickly become one of Australia's top ten bands .

Wa Wa Nee

This phenomenal band was formed in 1986. Their debut single 'Stimulation' and the subsequent, 'I Could Make You Love Me', gave them the status of being the first Australian band ever to have their first two singles in the National Top 10 simultaneously.

John Paul Young 1953–

In 1975 he and his band had enormous success with the hit song 'Yesterday's Hero'. He topped the European charts with 'Love is in the Air' and 'Standing in the Rain', in 1978.

Ballet and dance

Edouard Borovansky 1902–59

A ballet dancer, teacher and choreographer. He founded and directed the Borovansky Ballet, which formed the nucleus of the Australian Ballet Company.

Kelvin Coe 1946–

A dancer and foundation member of the Australian Ballet Company. As principal dancer, together with Marilyn Rowe Maver, he won a silver medal at the Moscow Ballet Competition in 1973.

Beth Dean (Carell) 1918–

An American-born dancer and choreographer, noted as an interpreter of Aboriginal music. Among her works is the ballet *Corroboree*, 1954.

Sir Robert Helpmann 1909–1986

An internationally renowned ballet dancer, choreographer, actor and director. He danced his way to fame in 1933, partnering Dame Margot Fonteyn at the Sadler's Wells ballet school.

Marilyn Jones 1940–

She is widely considered Australia's prima ballerina. She danced with the Marquis de Cuevas and Borovansky companies. She later became the artistic director of the Australian Ballet Company (1980–81).

Graeme Murphy 1950–

A Melbourne-born dancer and choreographer. He became the artistic director of the Sydney Dance Company in 1976 and is widely

---

DID YOU KNOW?

Marble Bar, Western Australia, recorded the longest period of extreme heat of above 37.7°C, for 160 days from October 1923 to April 1924.

acclaimed for his highly original works.

Dame Peggy van Praagh 1910—

A dancer and ballet mistress with the Sadler's Wells ballet school. She became the founding director of the Australian Ballet Company. In 1974 she was co-director with Sir Robert Helpmann.

Marilyn Rowe Maver 1946—

She is renowned as the first Australian ballerina to reach the pinnacle of her profession having trained only with the Australian Ballet Company. She won a silver medal in the 1973 Moscow Ballet Competition. Presently the director of the Australian Ballet Dance Company.

Roslyn Watson 1954—

A talented Aboriginal dancer who joined the Australian Dance Theatre in 1979. She had previous experience with the Dance Theatre of Harlem in 1973 and in 1976 she performed in the Third World Arts Festival held in Nigeria.

Garth Welch 1937—

A dancer, choreographer and teacher who is an advocate of abstract dance. He was invited to be a judge at the third International Ballet Competition in 1976.

Art

Davida Allen 1951—

She is a contemporary Queensland artist who has exhibited both nationally and internationally. Her paintings are mostly of people and she often uses her small daughters as subjects. Her portrait of Dr John Arthur McKelvie Shera won the Archibald Prize in 1986.

Suzanne Archer 1945—

A current and very active Sydney artist who is concerned with painting objects in her immediate surroundings. Her landscape 'Rock Pool Thirroul' won her the watercolour prize in the 1986 Archibald awards as well as The Pring Prize for the best female artist.

Judy Cassab 1920—

She was born in Vienna and came to Australia with her husband and two small sons as a refugee after the Second World War. She is best known as a portrait painter in an abstract and impressionist style. Her portraits of members of the royal family were hung at the Royal Academy in London in 1962.

John Coburn 1925—

An abstract painter, he was born in Queensland but has lived in Sydney since the

'The Rabbiters' by Russell Drysdale

Second World War. He painted *Valencia*, and designed the *Moon and Sun* curtains for the Sydney Opera House.

Grace Cossington Smith 1892–1984

She was a post-impressionist artist who began the first modern art school in Sydney. Her painting *The Sock Knitter*, 1915, was the first modern painting to be exhibited in Australia by an Australian.

Sir Russell Drysdale 1912–81

He was born in England into a family whose members had been among the pioneer pastoralists of Australia. *The Rabbiters* and *Sofala* are among his well-known works which capture the colour and people of the outback.

Sir William Dobell 1899–1970

His finest works were portraits such as *Dame Mary Gilmore* and *Margaret Olley*. He won the Archibald Prize in 1943 with a controversial painting of Joshua Smith. (The Archibald Prize was first awarded in 1921, and is given each year to the best portrait painted by an Australian artist.)

John Glover 1767–1849

Considered to be one of the most important colonial artists, he arrived in Tasmania in 1831, aged sixty-four. He recognised the differences and subtleties of light in Australia. Examples of his work include *Patterdale Farm* and *Glover's House and Garden*.

Sali Herman 1898–

Swiss-born, he came to Australia in 1937. He is best known for his pictures of the early slums and tenements of Sydney, particularly the areas of Paddington, Kings Cross and Woolloomooloo. Typical of his work are *Colonial Castle* and *Potts Point*.

Sir Hans Heysen 1877–1968

His parents emigrated from Germany to South Australia when he was 6 years old. He became a popular pastoral landscape artist.

Robert Klippel 1920–

He is considered to be our greatest modern contemporary sculptor. He has exhibited both nationally and internationally. His sculpture *Steel and Bronze*, 1961, is exhibited in the Sydney Art Gallery.

Norman Lindsay 1879–1969

A controversial and multi-talented artist, his works include woodcuts, watercolours and etchings. Well-known works are *Pollice Verso* and *The Crucified Venus*. He also wrote and illustrated the children's book *The Magic Pudding*.

Sir Bertram Mackennal 1863–1931

He was a prolific sculptor who studied and taught extensively overseas. Born in Melbourne he returned to that city in 1888 to complete panelling for Government House. His most famous works are *Circe*, 1893 (a figure in the round), a relief sculpture of Sarah Bernhardt, c 1893, and a marble bust of Dame Nellie Melba, 1899.

Conrad Martens 1801–78

An important colonial water-colourist, Martens left England in 1832. He sailed around the world for three years before settling in Sydney, where he painted numerous views of the harbour.

Frederick McCubbin 1855–1917

Inspired by the landscape around Melbourne, he painted many bush scenes portraying the early pioneers. His paintings include *Down on His Luck* 1889, *The Wallaby Track*

'Shearing the Rams' by Tom Roberts

1896 and the three-panelled work *The Pioneers* 1905.

Albert Namatjira 1902–59

A full-blooded member of the Arunta tribe, his water-colours of central Australia became very popular.

Sir Sydney Nolan 1917–

He is perhaps the most distinguished Australian painter of the century. He often painted series which together capture a changing mood or action. *Paradise Gardens,* consisting of 1320 paintings, was given by Nolan to the Victorian Arts Centre and is permanently housed in the Cultural Centre there. Other examples are the *Pretty Polly Mine* and *Ned Kelly* series.

John Olsen 1928–

A landscape painter of the emotions, his *Salute to Five Bells* can be seen in the Sydney Opera House. His *Spanish Encounter* is less well known.

Margaret Preston 1883–1963

A prolific painter, she was a forthright modernist who had an instinctive feel for colour. Late in her career she was influenced by Aboriginal art and carvings. Her works include *Implement Blue*, 1927, and *Gum Blossoms*, 1931.

Tom Roberts 1856–1931

He was known as 'the father of Australian landscape painting'. He and Frederick McCubbin formed the famous painting camps of the Heidelberg School, in Melbourne. Later they were joined by Charles Conder and Arthur Streeton. These men became Australia's first national painters, capturing at last the spirit and colour of the Australian landscape. Tom Roberts's national paintings include *Bailed Up, Shearing the Rams* and *The Golden Fleece*.

Dick Roughsey c 1920–

A member of the Lardil tribe from the Gulf of Carpentaria. He was encouraged to paint by a charter pilot, Percy Trezise, and his works have been exhibited in Cairns, Brisbane and Canberra, where he has achieved considerable acclaim. His paintings include selections from his book *The Rainbow Serpent*, 1976.

Tim Storrier 1950–

A contemporary abstract painter, he is an exponent of still-life paintings. His works include *Moonstick, Box and Berry—Still Life with Fire*, 1976, and *Isolation*, 1977.

Sir Arthur Streeton (1867–1943)

He was revered as the painter who 'fixed the image of his country'. He was a First World War official artist and his works are displayed in the Australian War Memorial in Canberra. He is noted for his paintings *Fire's On, Lapstone Tunnel* and *The Purple Moon's Transparent Might*.

The Sunny South' by Tom Roberts

Ron Robertson Swan 1941–

He is a contemporary surrealist sculptor who works with unemotional objects. His machine-like sculpture *Big Red* was executed in 1962.

Clifford Possum Tjapaltjarri and Tim Leura Tjapaltjarri

They are Aboriginal painters, members of the Annatjira clan of the Northern Territory, who in the 1960s and 1970s learnt to use the contemporary mediums of acrylic and canvas. Their paintings include traditional symbols and imagery but they are painted in a contemporary way. An example of their art *Paint on Canvas—Warlugulong*, 1976, is hanging in the Sydney Art Gallery.

Brett Whiteley 1939–

He is an uninhibited and polished draftsman, who tries to express the 'life force and its insoluble conflicts'. His works include *The Christie Series*, *The Big Orange* and *The Balcony*.

Fred Williams 1927–82

Born in Melbourne, in his works he simplified and abstracted the landscape. Examples include *You Yangs* and *Waterfall Polyptych*.

Sporting highlights

1901 Australia defeats England in second test match in Melbourne. M A Noble takes seven wickets for 17 runs.

1902 Australia defeats England 2–1 in 1901–02 series test cricket.

1903 First car race in Australia. Dick Cavill wins every men's freestyle event at Australian swimming championships.

1904 First Australian Open golf championship held at Botany (New South Wales).

1905 First Davis Cup entry by Australasia.

1906 Bondi Surf Bathers' Life Saving Club is formed.

1907 First Davis Cup win to Australasia. Norman Brookes is the first non-British tennis player to win a Wimbledon title. Rugby League football begins.

1908 First Australian Surf Carnival held at Manly. Hugh D McIntosh builds Sydney Stadium to promote world boxing.

1912 The all-round sportsman 'Snowy' Baker buys Sydney Stadium and establishes championship conditions, rules and standardisation in Australian boxing. Jerry Jerome becomes first Aboriginal to hold the title of national boxing champion. Fanny Durack (for 100 metres freestyle) wins Australia's first ever Olympic gold medal at Stockholm Olympics.

1913 Dally Messenger, 'master of Australian Rugby League', retires.

1914 Norman Brookes wins men's singles tennis title at Wimbledon.

1916 Les Darcy becomes Australian heavyweight boxing champion.

1917 Annette Kellerman makes world record dive of 28 metres. Les Darcy dies in the United States.

1919 Australian Imperial Force rowing team wins Royal Henley Peace Regatta — the trophy becomes the King's Cup.

1922 Gerald Patterson wins men's singles tennis title at Wimbledon.

1924 Australia wins three gold medals at Paris Olympics. Andrew 'Boy' Charlton (1500 metres freestyle), Anthony Winter (triple jump), Dick Eve (high dive). Speedway racing is inaugurated at Maitland, New South Wales.

1926 Roy Cazaly becomes folk-hero of Australian Rules football. The cry 'Up there Cazaly' passes into the language.

1927 First meeting of 'electric hare racing' at Epping, New South Wales.

1928 H R Pearce wins gold medal at Amsterdam Olympics for single sculls rowing. Don Bradman plays in his first cricket test match. Hubert Opperman wins French Bol d'Or 24-hour cycling event.

1929 Sydney–Perth Trans-Continental Air Race — de Havilland makes fastest time in *Gypsy Moth*. Bradman sets world record in first class cricket for a single innings with a score of 452 runs.

1930 Phar Lap wins Melbourne Cup, at 11/8 on, being the shortest odds in history of Cup. Bradman's aggregate of 974 runs in five tests against England sets world record (still stands) of 139.14.

1932 Phar Lap dies in the United States in controversial circumstances. Walter Lindrum sets world record in billiards. 'Bodyline' cricket test series begins. Australia wins three gold medals at Los Angeles Olympics. Claire Dennis (200 metres breaststroke), Duncan Gray (cycling), H R Pearce (rowing).

1933 England regains the Ashes after controversial 'bodyline' cricket tour.

1934 C W A Scott and T Campbell Black win Melbourne Centenary England–Australia Air Race.

1935 Adrian Quist and Jack Crawford win Wimbledon doubles title.

The Melbourne Cup

1936 Don Bradman appointed Australian cricket captain. Lionel van Praag wins first world speedway title. Water-skiing begins in Australia. No Australians win gold medals at Berlin Olympics.

1937 First Australian women cricketers tour England.

1938 Bathurst's Mt Panorama racing circuit completed. Peter Whitehead of England wins Grand Prix at Bathurst.

1939 Australia wins Davis Cup for first time.

1945 First Sydney–Hobart yacht race.

1946 Sydney Turf Club introduces photo-finish cameras. Horace Lindrum wins world snooker championship.

1947 Jim Ferrier wins title of United States professional golf champion. John Marshall wins every Australian men's freestyle championship.

1948 Australia wins two gold medals in London Olympics. John Winter (high jump), Mervyn Wood (single sculls). Don Bradman retires from test cricket with an aggregate of 6996 runs made in 52 tests (Av 99.9).

1949 Don Bradman is knighted. David Sands wins Empire middleweight boxing title.

1950 Jockey Rae 'Togo' Johnstone wins four of the five England classic horse races in one season. Adrian Quist and John Bromwich win Wimbledon doubles title. John Marshall causes a sensation in the United States at the national swimming championships when he wins three titles and establishes four world freestyle records. Clive Churchill captains Australia's Rugby League team to victory against England.

1951 Frank Sedgman wins United States men's singles tennis title.

1952 Australia wins six gold medals at Helsinki Olympics. Marjorie Jackson (100 metres and 200 metres), Shirley Strickland (80 metres hurdles), Russell Mockridge (cycling), Mockridge–Lionel Cox (tandem). Ken Rosewall and Lew Hoad (both 17) win Wimbledon doubles tennis. Jimmy Carruthers is Australia's second world boxing champion.

1953 Lew Hoad and Ken Rosewall retain Davis Cup.

1954 Golfers Peter Thompson and Kel Nagle win Canada Cup. Peter Thompson wins the British Open golf tournament.

DID YOU KNOW?

The racecourse Automatic Totalizator (tote) was invented by George Julius of Sydney in 1913.

Jimmy Carruthers retires undefeated from world boxing. John Landy becomes the second man to break the four minute mile — a few weeks after Roger Bannister of England. Bannister beats Landy at Vancouver Commonwealth Games (the first race where two men break the four minute mile). Clive Churchill captains Australian World Cup Rugby League team in France. 'Gelignite' Jack Murray wins Redex Motor Trial.

1955 Arthur 'Scobie' Breasley begins a horse-racing record of 100 winners each season.

1956 The first Olympic Games held in the Southern Hemisphere are held in Melbourne. Australia wins 13 gold medals. Betty Cuthbert (100 metres and 200 metres), Shirley Strickland (80 metres hurdles), women's relay, Ian Brown and Anthony Marchant (cycling), Jon Hendricks (100 metres freestyle), Murray Rose (400 metres freestyle and 1500 metres freestyle), David Thiele (100 metres backstroke), men's swimming relay, Dawn Fraser (100 metres freestyle), Lorraine Crapp (400 metres freestyle), and women's swimming relay. Lew Hoad beats Ken Rosewall for men's singles tennis title at Wimbledon. Peter Thompson wins the British Open golf tournament, the first Australian to win the event three years in succession.

Aussie Rules Football

1957 Ian Craig captains Australia's cricket team in
Johannesburg. John Marshall, the swimmer, is killed in a
car crash. Ron Barassi kicks five goals in Australian Rules
grand final match between Melbourne and Essendon.

1958 Herb Elliott runs his first sub-four-minute mile in 3 minutes
59.9 seconds. Marlene Matthews sets world records for
running 90 metres and 200 metres. Richie Benaud, great
all-rounder, captains Australian cricket team from 1958 to
1963.

1959 Racing driver Jack Brabham becomes world Grand Prix
champion. Reg Gasnier begins his career in Rugby League.
John Konrads wins all men's freestyle swimming events in
the Australian championships.

1960 Australia wins eight gold medals at the Rome Olympics.
Herb Elliott (1500 metres, a world record), Dawn Fraser
(100 metres freestyle), Murray Rose (400 metres freestyle),
David Thiele (100 metres backstroke), John Devitt (100
metres freestyle), John Konrads (1500 metres freestyle)
and two in the equestrian events. Neale Frazer beats Rod
Laver at Wimbledon. Australia plays the West Indies in the
only cricket test ever tied. Kel Nagle wins British Open golf
championship in its centenary year.

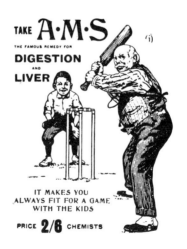

TAKE A·M·S

THE FAMOUS REMEDY FOR

DIGESTION

AND

LIVER

IT MAKES YOU
ALWAYS FIT FOR A GAME
WITH THE KIDS

PRICE **2/6** CHEMISTS

1961 Heather Blundell McKay is national squash champion.
1962 Australia wins 17 gold medals in the Perth Commonwealth Games. *Gretel* challenges for America's Cup (loses 4–1). Dawn Fraser becomes the first woman swimmer to break 60 seconds for 100 metres freestyle. Rod Laver wins 'Grand Slam' of world tennis, becoming the second man to do so. Stewart McKenzie wins Henley Diamond Sculls for the sixth time. Reg Gasnier is appointed Australia's youngest-ever Rugby League test captain (aged 23).
1963 Margaret Smith Court is first Australian to win Wimbledon women's singles title. Ken Hiscoe wins all world squash titles. Australian netball team wins world championship in London.
1964 The first official world surfing championship held at Manly, won by Midget Farrelly. Australia wins six gold medals at the Tokyo Olympics. Betty Cuthbert (400 metres), Dawn Fraser (100 metres freestyle), Kevin Berry (200 metres butterfly), Ian O'Brien (200 metres breaststroke), Robert Windle (1500 metres freestyle), and the 5.5 metre class yachting team. Dawn Fraser becomes the first and only swimmer, male or female, to win gold medals in three successive Olympic Games (still stands).
1965 Linda McGill is the first Australian to swim the English Channel. Long-distance runner Ron Clarke breaks 11 world records. Geoff Hunt is national squash champion at 17 years of age. George Moore wins his eighth consecutive Sydney jockeys' premiership. Peter Thompson wins the British Open golf tournament for the fifth time (he is second only to H Vardon who won it six times).
1966 First-ever lawn bowls world championships held in Sydney. Australia wins.
1967 Australia wins Admiral's Cup for yachting. Australia wins Davis Cup for the fourth successive time. Roy Emerson becomes Australian singles tennis champion. *Dame Pattie* loses America's Cup challenge. George Moore wins the English Derby on Royal Palace.
1968 Australia wins five gold medals at the Mexico Olympics. Ralph Doubell (800 metres), Maureen Caird (80 metres hurdles), Michael Wenden (100 and 200 metres freestyle), Lynette McClements (100 metres butterfly). Annual Iron Man surfing championships introduced. Barry Rogers wins first three. Boxer Lionel Rose wins world bantamweight title. Rod Laver becomes the first player to win two 'Grand

Slams' in world tennis. Nat Young wins world surfboard championship.

1969 Boxer Johnny Famechon wins world featherweight title. Margaret Court wins 'Grand Slam' of tennis (only the second woman to do so).

1970 Australia loses third America's Cup challenge. John Newcombe wins men's singles at Wimbledon. Judy Trim wins world championship in ladies' standard pistol shooting. Bill Lawry retires from test cricket after scoring a total of 13 centuries. Ken Rosewall wins USA open tennis championship.

1971 Wayne Jones is the first Australian to waterski over 160 km/h. Australia excels at Wimbledon with wins to John Newcombe (men's singles), Roy Emerson and Rod Laver (men's doubles) and Evonne Goolagong, the first Aboriginal to play at Wimbledon, women's singles. Three noted cricketers begin their careers: Greg Chappell, Dennis Lillee and Rodney Marsh. Australian netball team wins the world championship in Kingston, Jamaica. Gunsynd, the 'Goondiwindi grey', wins the 'grand slam' of four top mile events in Australian horse racing — the Epsom, Toorak, George Adams and Doncaster handicaps.

1972 Australia wins eight gold medals at Munich Olympics. Brad Cooper (400 metres freestyle), Shane Gould (200 metres individual medley, 400 metres freestyle, 200 metres freestyle — all world records), Beverley Whitfield (200 metres breaststroke), Gail Neall (400 metres individual medley) and two for yachting. Shane Gould becomes the first woman to hold all world freestyle swimming records at once (five). Joe Meissner, from Sydney, becomes the first non-Japanese world karate champion.

1973 Margaret Court wins her fifth United States tennis singles championship. Heather McKay wins her fourteenth Australian women's squash title. Australia qualifies for World Soccer Cup final for first time. Australian netball team wins world championship in Auckland, New Zealand.

1974 Evonne Goolagong wins Australian women's open tennis title. Des Renford, aged 40, becomes 'King of the Channel' with his tenth crossing. His final tally for his career is 19 crossing swims. Raylene Boyle wins three gold medals at the Commonwealth Games in Christchurch, New Zealand.

1975 John Newcombe wins Australian men's open tennis title.

1976 No Australian wins gold medals at Montreal Olympics.

1977 Women's bowls team wins a gold medal in world bowls titles. Heather McKay wins her sixteenth British squash championship title, which is regarded as a world supremacy record. David Graham wins Australian Open golf championship. Rocky Mattioli wins the world junior middleweight boxing championship. Trainer Bart Cummings has his sixth Melbourne Cup win with the horse Gold and Black. World Series Cricket is launched. Australia and England commemorate 100 years of test cricket. Wayne Bartholomew wins world surfing championship.

1978 Tracey Wickham takes the only world record set at the Commonwealth Games with her swim in the 800 metres. Australian women's cricket team wins the second World Cup tournament in India. Ken Warby sets world's water speed record. Edwina Kennedy, 19, of Sydney, becomes British women's amateur golf champion.

1979 Jack Newton wins Australian Open golf tournament.

1980 Australia wins two gold medals at the Moscow Olympic Games. Michelle Ford (800 metres freestyle) and the men's 4 x 100 medley relay. Greg Norman wins Australian Open golf tournament. Geoff Hunt wins his seventh Australian Open squash title. Grant Kenny wins both junior and senior Iron Man titles, at 16 years of age. Alan Jones wins world's Formula One racing car driver championship.

1981 David Graham wins United States Open golf championship. Tommy Smith wins his thirtieth successive horse trainer's premiership. Australian women's cricket team wins third World Cup tournament in New Zealand. Jan Stephenson wins the women's world golfing championship in Japan.

1982 Commonwealth Games held in Brisbane. Gold medals to Lisa Curry (400 metres medley), Robert de Castella (marathon), Raylene Boyle (400 metres). Bob Shearer wins Australian Open golf tournament. Kangaroo Rugby League team wins all matches against British Isles and France, for the first time.

1983 Cliff Young at 61 wins the inaugural Sydney to Melbourne ultra-marathon. Jeanette Baker wins World Cup for tenpin bowling. Greg Chappell retires. He was Australia's highest run-getter with 7110 runs in his career, played in over 90 tests. Dennis Lillee retires — considered the greatest wicket-taker in world test cricket. Rodney Marsh retires as one of the greatest wicketkeepers of all time. Steven Lee ranks among top twenty world skiers in downhill racing events. *Australia II* wins the America's Cup for 12 metre class yachting, after America had held it for 132 years. Eddie Charlton considered the top snooker player in the world after winning a number of national and international titles over a period of twenty years. Grant Kenny wins his fourth successive senior Iron Man title.

1984 Australia wins four gold medals at the Los Angeles Olympics. Dean Lukin (weightlifting in super heavyweight), Glynis Nunn (heptathlon), Jon Sieben (200 metres butterfly), and cycling team in 4000 metres men's pursuit. Peter Brock wins Bathurst 1000 car race for eighth time. Kim Hughes, captain of Australia's cricket team, resigns over criticisms of his captaincy against West Indies. The Wallabies Rugby Union team are undefeated and complete a 'grand slam' by defeating England, Scotland, Wales and Ireland in four tests. Mark Ella is the first Aboriginal to become captain of Australian Rugby Union team (1982–3). On the Wallabies' tour to United Kingdom he scores tries against England, Wales, Scotland and Ireland — all in the one season (a record).

DID YOU KNOW?

The average Australian can expect to eat during his or her lifetime: 17 beef cattle, 92 sheep, 406 loaves of bread, 165 000 eggs, half a tonne of cheese, 8 tonnes of fruit, and 10 tonnes of vegetables.

1985 Inaugural Australia Games held. Three Australian boxers win world titles. Jeff Fenech (at 20) wins IBF world bantamweight title, Lester Ellis wins IBF junior lightweight title and Barry Michael then wins IBF junior lightweight title from Ellis. An Australian rebel cricket team tours South Africa. The Australian women's bowls team wins three gold medals at World Bowls titles held in Melbourne. World Formula One Grand Prix first held in Adelaide.

1986 Robert de Castella wins the Boston Marathon. Australia wins 40 gold medals in the Edinburgh Commonwealth Games. These include Lisa Martin's win in the inaugural women's marathon and Gail Martin's first Australian win in the women's discus and shot putt. For the second time running, the Kangaroo Rugby League team is undefeated in tour of British Isles and France.

1987 Greg Norman wins British Open Golf Championship. Jeff Fenech wins the EBC World Super Bantamweight Boxing Championship, thus becoming the first Australian to win recognition as world champion in two divisions. Wayne Gardner wins the World 500 cc Motorcycle Championship. Pat Cash becomes first Australian to win Wimbledon Tennis Championship in 17 years.

Books

This is a selection of much-loved Australian books. Many have won national and international literary awards and so deserve to be included. Others are great favourites which most Australians have on their bookshelf and regard as old friends.

Title	Author	Publisher	Year
Anzac's	Pasty Adam-Smith	Nelson	1978
Bushwacker's Australian Song Book, The	J Wositzky and D Newton	Anne O'Donovan	1982
Damned Whores and God's Police	A Summers	Penguin	1975
Education of Young Donald, The	Donald Horne	Penguin	1975
Falling Towards England	Clive James	Picador	1985
Flaws in the Glass	Patrick White	Penguin	1980
Fortunate Life, A	A B Facey	Penguin	1981
From Curtin to Hawke	Fred Daley	Sun	1984
Growing Up in . . . (series)	A T Yarwood	Kangaroo Press	1984
Let Stalk Strine	Afferbeck Lauder	Lansdowne Rigby	1982
Letters of Rachel Henning, The	David Adams(ed.)	Nelson	1979
Lily on the Dustbin	Nancy Keesing	Penguin	1982
Lucky Country, The	D Horne	A & R	1978
Macquarie Dictionary, The		The Macquarie Library	1981
Man in the Red Turban	David Martin	Penguin	1978
Million Wild Acres, A	Eric Rolls	Penguin	1981
Mother Stayed at Home	Gwen Badgery	James Fraser	1985
My Wife, My Daughter and Poor Mary Anne	B Kingston	Nelson	1977
One Man's War	Stan Arneil	Alternative Publishing Company	1978
Oxford Anthology of Australian Literature	Leonie Kramer and Adrian Mitchell (eds)	Oxford University Press	1985
Oxford History of Australia, Vol. 4		Oxford University Press	1986
Penguin Leunig, The	Michael Leunig	Penguin	1974
Presenting Australia	D Conlon	Child & Henry	1981
Real Matilda, The	Miriam Dixson	Penguin	1976
Short History of Australia, A	Manning Clark	Macmillan	1981
Snow on the Saltbush	G Dutton	Penguin	1984

Sons in the Saddle and Kings in Grass Castles	Mary Durack	Constable	1959
Tales of the Old and New	Elsie Roughsey	Penguin	1984
Taste of Australia, A	P Taylor	Pan	1980
Triumph of the Nomads	G Blainey	Macmillan	1975
Trucanini, Queen or Traitor?	Vivienne Rae Ellis	Australian Institute of Aboriginal Studies	1981
Tyranny of Distance, The	G Blainey	Sun Books	1966
Unreliable Memoirs	Clive James	Picador	1980
Unspeakable Adams	Phillip Adams	Nelson	1977
Watcher on the Cast Iron Balcony	Hal Porter	Faber & Faber	1971
Weevils in the Flour	W Lowenstein	Hyland House	1978

Fiction

All the Rivers Run	Nancy Cato	New English Library	1978
Battlers and Come in Spinner	Kylie Tennant	Penguin	1941 and 1967
Capricornia	Xavier Herbert	Shillington House	1981
Cassidy	Morris West	Hodder & Stoughton	1986
Chant of Jimmie Blacksmith, The	Thomas Keneally	Fontana	1972
Coonardoo	Katharine Susannah Prichard	A & R	1975
Everlasting Secret Family and Other Secrets, The	Frank Moorhouse	A & R	1980
For the Term of His Natural Life	Marcus Clarke	Currey O'Neill	1981
Fortunes of Richard Mahony, The	Henry Handel Richardson	Penguin	1982
Harp in the South	Ruth Park	Penguin	1948
House is Built, A	M Barnard Eldershaw	Lloyd O'Neill	1972
Illywhacker	Peter Carey	University of Queensland Press	1985

Johnno	David Malouf	University of Queensland Press	1975
Man Who Loved Children, The	Christina Stead	Penguin	1979
Mango Tree, The	Ronald McKie	Collins	1974
My Brilliant Career	Miles Franklin	A & R	1979
My Brother Jack	George Johnston	Collins	1981
On Our Selection	Steele Rudd	A & R	1973
Picnic at Hanging Rock	Joan Lindsay	Cheshire Publishing	1967
Poor Fellow My Country	Xavier Herbert	Fontana	1975
Power Without Glory	Frank Hardy	A & R	1982
Redheap	Norman Lindsay	A & R	1979
Robbery Under Arms	Rolf Boldrewood	Currey O'Neil	1980
Sara Dane	Catherine Gaskin	Collins	1955
Shiralee	D'Arcy Niland	A & R	1980
Sundowners	John Cleary	A & R	1980
They're a Weird Mob	J O'Grady	Landsdowne	1981
Thorn Birds, The	Colleen McCullough	Harper	1977
Timeless Land, The	Eleanor Dark	A & R	1980
Town Like Alice, A	Neville Shute	Heinemann	1950
Transit of Venus, The	Shirley Hazzard	Penguin	1980
Tree of Man, The	Patrick White	Penguin	1973
Voss	Patrick White	Penguin	1960
While the Billy Boils	Henry Lawson	Currey O'Neill	1980
Woman of the Future, A	David Ireland	Penguin	1979

Poetry

Around the Boree Log	John O'Brien	A & R	1921
Collected Poems	A D Hope	A & R	1975
Collected Poems	James McAuley	A & R	1971
Collected Poems	Judith Wright	A & R	1971
Collected Verse	A B Paterson	A & R	1982
Dimensions (anthology)	Bruce Dawe (ed)	McGraw-Hill	1974
Joe Wilson's Mates	Henry Lawson	Currey O'Neill	1980
Man From Snowy River and Other Verses	A B Paterson	A & R	1982
My People (anthology)	Kath Walker	Jacaranda Wiley	1981
Passionate Heart and Other Poems	Dame Mary Gilmore	A & R	1979

Penguin Book of Australian Verse, The	H Heseltine (ed)	Penguin	1982
Poetic Works of Henry Lawson, The	Henry Lawson	A & R	1981
Selected Poems	Kenneth Slessor	A & R	1975
Selected Poems	Gwen Harwood	A & R	1975
Selected Poems	Rosemary Dobson	A & R	1975
Selected Poems	Douglas Stewart	A & R	1937
Sentimental Bloke, The	C J Dennis	A & R	1977
Treasury of Colonial Poetry, The		Currawong Press	1982
Vernacular Republic, The	Les Murray	A & R	1976

Drama

Club, The	David Williamson	Currency Press	1978
Don's Party	David Williamson	Currency Press	1973
Elocution of Benjamin Franklin, The	Steve J Spears	Currency Press	1977
Fire on the Snow, The	Douglas Stewart	A & R	1976
Hard God, A	Peter Kenna	Currency Press	1974
Norm and Ahmed	Alexander Buzo	Currency Press	1976
One Day of the Year, The	Alan Seymour	A &R	1976
Removalists, The	David Williamson	Currency Press	1972
Rusty Bugles	Sumner Locke Elliot	Currency Press	1980
Shifting Heart, The	R Beynon	A & R	1976
Summer of the Seventeenth Doll	Ray Lawler	Currency Press	1978

Books for children

Amy's Place	M Stafford	Nelson	1980
Ash Road	I Southall	A & R	1985
Blue Fin	C Thiele	Rigby	1982
Chai	Pam Blashki and Clifton Pugh	Heinemann	1985
Cole's Funny Picture Book	E W Cole	Collins	1984
Complete Adventures of Blinky Bill, The	Dorothy Wall	A & R	1985

Complete Adventures of Snugglepot and Cuddlepie	May Gibbs	A & R	1963
Dot and the Kangaroo	Ethel Pedley	A & R	1978
Fire in the Stone	C Thiele	Penguin	1981
Gulpilil's Stories of the Dreamtime	H Rule and S Goodman	Collins	1979
I Can Jump Puddles	Alan Marshall	Allen Lane	1981
Illalong Children, The	A B Paterson	Lansdowne	1984
Little Black Princess, The	Mrs Aeneas Gunn	A & R	1982
Little Bush Maid	Mary Grant Bruce	Ward Lock	1974
Magic Pudding, The	Norman Lindsay	A & R	1977
Seven Little Australians	Ethel Turner	Ward Lock	1894
Storm Boy	C Thiele	Penguin	1981
Waltzing Matilda (children's illustrated version)	A B Paterson	Collins	1970
Wild Colonial Boy, The (children's illustrated version)	J A King	Collins	1985
We of the Never Never	Mrs Aeneas Gunn	A & R	1982

Films

Take 1: silent films

Since 1970 we have experienced an extraordinary upsurge of world-wide interest in Australian films. However, our film industry dates back to the late 1890s.

Here is a brief selection of films from some producers and directors who pioneered the industry in those early days. They helped to engender a spirit of cohesiveness and nationalism in the people of a vast and scattered land.

Date	Film title	Producer or director
1898	Our Social Triumphs	Salvation Army Films
1900	Soldiers of the Cross	Salvation Army Films
1906	The Story of the Kelly Gang	J & N Tait
1907	Robbery Under Arms	J & N Tait
1911	Captain Midnight	Charles Cozens Spencer
1916	Mutiny on the Bounty	Raymond Longford
1919	The Sentimental Bloke	Raymond Longford

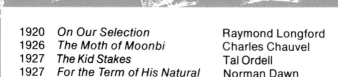

1920	*On Our Selection*	Raymond Longford
1926	*The Moth of Moonbi*	Charles Chauvel
1927	*The Kid Stakes*	Tal Ordell
1927	*For the Term of His Natural Life*	Norman Dawn

Take II: the talkies

For thirty years the Australian film industry was in eclipse, and Australians, like other people all over the world, flocked to see the products of Hollywood. However, some Australian films had popular success.

Date	Film title	Producer or director
1933	*The Squatter's Daughter*	Ken Hall
1940	*Forty Thousand Horsemen*	Charles Chauvel
1949	*The Rats of Tobruk*	Charles Chauvel
1949	*Sons of Matthew*	Charles Chauvel
1949	*Eureka Stockade*	Harry Watt
1951	*Captain Thunderbolt*	Cecil Holmes
1955	*Jedda*	Charles Chauvel
1958	*Smiley*	Anthony Kimmins
1966	*They're A Weird Mob*	Michael Powell
1969	*Age of Consent*	Michael Powell

Take III: the 1970s surge

During the 1970s the Australian film industry expanded greatly, and produced a number of films which won international acclaim. Here is a selection of the most successful box-office hits.
Key: P = producer, D = director, A = actor

Date	Film title	Producers, Directors, Actors
1971	*Wake in Fright*	George Willoughby (P), Ted Kotcheff (D), Garry Bond (A)
1972	*The Adventures of Barry McKenzie*	Phillip Adams (P), Barry Crocker (A)
1973	*Alvin Purple*	Tim Burstall (D), Graeme Blundell (A)
1974	*The Cars that Ate Paris*	Peter Weir (D), Terri Camilleri (A)
1975	*Picnic at Hanging Rock*	Pat Lovell (P), Anne Lambert (A)

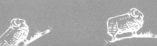

1975	*The Removalists*	Margaret Fink (P), John Hargreaves (A)
1975	*Sunday Too Far Away*	Gil Brealey (P), Jack Thompson (A)
1976	*Caddie*	Donald Crombie (P), Helen Morse (A)
1976	*Don's Party*	Phillip Adams (P), John Hargreaves (A)
1976	*The Devil's Playground*	Fred Schepisi (D), Arthur Dignam (A)
1976	*Storm Boy*	Matt Carroll (P), Greg Rowe (A), Henri Safran (D)
1976	*The Fourth Wish* (TV)	Don Chaffey (D), John Meillon (A)
1977	*The Getting of Wisdom*	Phillip Adams (P), Susannah Fowler (A)
1978	*My Brilliant Career*	Gillian Armstrong (D), Judy Davis (A)
1978	*Newsfront*	Phillip Noyce (D), David Elfick (P), Bill Hunter (A)
1978	*The Chant of Jimmie Blacksmith*	Fred Schepisi (D), Tommy Lewis (A)
1979	*Mad Max I*	George Miller (P), Mel Gibson (A)
1979	*Breaker Morant*	Bruce Beresford (D), Jack Thompson (A)

Take IV: Films of the 1980s

Date	Film title	Producers, Directors, Actors
1981	*Winter of Our Dreams*	John Duigan (D), Richard Mason (P), Judy Davis (A), Bryan Brown (A)
1982	*Gallipoli*	Pat Lovell (P), Peter Weir (D), Mel Gibson (A), Mark Lee (A)
1982	*The Man from Snowy River*	Geoff Burrowes (P), George Miller (D), Tom Burlinson (A)
1983	*Careful He Might Hear You*	Jill Robb (P), Wendy Hughes (A), John Hargreaves (A)
1983	*Phar Lap*	Simon Winser (D), Tom Burlinson (A)
1983	*The Year of Living Dangerously*	Peter Weir (D), Mel Gibson (A), Linda Hunt (A)
1984	*Coolangatta Gold*	John Weiley (P), Igor Auzins (D), Colin Friels (A), Nick Tate (A)
1984	*My First Wife*	Jane Ballantyne (P), Paul Cox (P and D), John Hargreaves (A)

1984	*Robbery Under Arms*	Jock Blair (P), Sam Neill (A)
1984	*Silver City*	John Long (P), Sophia Turkiewicz (D), Ivor Kants (A), Gosia Dobrowolska (A)
1985	*Mad Max: Beyond Thunderdome*	George Ogilvie (D), George Miller (D and P), John Sexton (P), Mel Gibson (A)
1985	*Burke and Wills*	Graeme Clifford (P and D), Jack Thompson (A), Nigel Havers (A)
1985	*Empty Beach*	Tim Read (P), Chris Thompson (D), Bryan Brown (A)
1985	*Bliss*	Ray Lawrence (D), Tony Buckley (P), Barry Otto (A)
1986	*Crocodile Dundee*	Peter Faiman (D), Paul Hogan (A)
1986	*Cactus*	Paul Cox (D), Isabelle Huppert (A), Robert Menzies (A)
1986	*For Love Alone*	Stephen Wallace (D), Helen Buday (A), Hugo Weaving (A), Sam Neill (A)
1986	*The Fringe Dwellers*	Bruce Beresford (D), Kristina Nehm (A), Justine Saunders (A)
1986	*The More Things Change*	Robyn Nevin (D), Victoria Longley (A), Barry Otto (A)
1986	*Backlash*	Bill Bennett (P & D), David Argue (A), Gia Carides (A)
1986	*Devil in the Flesh*	Scott Murray (D), Katia Caballero (A), Keith Smith (A)
1987	*The Place at the Coast*	George Ogilvie (D), John Hargreaves (A), Heather Mitchell (A)
1987	*Ground Zero*	Michael Pattinson (D), Colin Friels (A), Jack Thompson (A)
1987	*Les Patterson Saves the World*	George Miller (D), Barry Humphries (A), Pamela Stephenson (A)
1987	*Shadows of the Peacock*	Phillip Noyce (D), Wendy Hughes (A)
1987	*High Tide*	Gillian Armstrong (D), Judy Davis (A), Colin Friels (A)
1987	*The Lighthorsemen*	Simon Wincer (P & D), Peter Philps (A), Jon Blake (A), Sigrid Thornton (A)

Songs and poems

Advance Australia Fair

The original words and music were supposedly written and composed by Peter Dodds McCormick about 1878. In 1983 a new version of the song was adopted by the Australian government as the national anthem.

Australians all let us rejoice,
For we are young and free,
We've golden soil and wealth
    for toil;
Our home is girt by sea;
Our land abounds in
    nature's gifts
Of beauty rich and rare;
In history's page,
    let every stage
Advance Australia Fair.

Beneath our radiant Southern
    Cross,
We'll toil with hearts and

hands;
To make this Commonwealth
    of ours
Renowned of all the lands;
For those who've come
    across the seas
We've boundless plains
    to share
With courage let us all
    combine
To Advance Australia Fair.
In joyful strains then
    let us sing,
Advance Australia Fair.

This is a song about a swagman, a wanderer, who roams the outback of Australia. The only comfort he has against the harsh life on the track is his 'Matilda', a blanket roll. He is not beyond claiming for himself a stray jumbuck or two, but as graziers are aware of sheep-stealing practices, he is soon caught. He is arrested, but as the troopers are about to cart him off, he jumps into the billabong. From the reedy depths of the water he defies the law, making it clear that he would rather die by drowning than be taken prisoner.

However, 'Waltzing Matilda' is far more than a song about a crafty swaggie. It universally marks us as Australian, and is a song which seems to embody the rebellious spirit of early Australia, reminding us of the harsh beginnings of white settlement. It is a song which evokes great emotion and which lives in the hearts of most Australians.

Once a jolly swagman
   camped by a billabong,
Under the shade of a
   coolabah tree,
And he sang as he watched
   and waited till his billy
   boiled,
'Who'll come a-waltzing
   Matilda with me?'

Chorus

'Waltzing Matilda, waltzing
   Matilda,
'Who'll come a-waltzing
   Matilda with me?'
And he sang as he watched
   and waited till his billy
   boiled,
'Who'll come a-waltzing
   Matilda with me?'

Down came a jumbuck to
   drink at the billabong,
Up jumped the swagman and
   grabbed him with glee,

And he sang as he shoved
   that jumbuck in his
   tuckerbag,
'You'll come a-waltzing
   Matilda with me'.

Up rode the squatter mounted
   on his thoroughbred,
Down came the troopers, one,
   two, three,
'Where's that jolly jumbuck
   you've got in your
   tuckerbag?
You'll come a-waltzing
   Matilda with me'.

Up jumped the swagman and
   jumped into that billabong,
'You'll never take me alive',
   said he.
And his ghost may be heard
   as you pass by that
   billabong:
'Who'll come a-waltzing
   Matilda with me?'

This song typifies the strong camaraderie which exists in the shearing sheds of Australia.

Shearing is back-breaking work, requiring a high level of skill and physical fitness. The 'ringer' is the champion shearer and he is constantly being challenged by his mates, especially by the 'snaggers', the old men of the shed, who are past their prime. To beat the 'ringer' would be a feather in their caps. Of course, to do this sometimes involves taking short cuts, such as choosing a ewe with no belly wool or not shearing close enough to the skin. This would put the old-timer at a distinct advantage. Naturally the grazier-landowner is ever watchful for shoddy workmanship, so the snagger has to be quite crafty.

As the work in the shed comes to a halt, the shearers go off to the nearest pub, to quench their thirsts with their mates. Obviously their philosophy is: work hard, drink hard and die hard.

Out on the board the old
   shearer stands,
Grasping his shears in his
   long, bony hands;
Fixed is his gaze on a bare-
   bellied ewe,
Glory if he gets her, won't he
   make the ringer go!

Chorus

Click go the shears boys,
   click, click, click;
Wide is his blow and his
   hands move quick,
The ringer looks round and is
   beaten by a blow,
And curses the old snagger
   with the bare-bellied ewe.

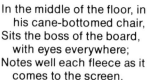

In the middle of the floor, in
  his cane-bottomed chair,
Sits the boss of the board,
  with eyes everywhere;
Notes well each fleece as it
  comes to the screen,
Paying strict attention if it's
  taken off clean.

The tar-boy is there, awaiting
  in demand,
With his blackened tar-pot,
  and his tarry hand,
Sees one old sheep with a cut
  upon its back,
Hears what he's waiting for,
  'Tar here, Jack!'

Shearing is all over and we've
  all got our cheques.
Roll up your swag boys, we're
  off on the tracks;
The first pub we come to, it's
there we'll have a spree,
And everyone that comes
  along, it's 'Have a drink
  with me!'

Down by the bar the old
  shearer stands,
Grasping his glass in his thin
  bony hands;
Fixed is his gaze on the
  green-painted keg,
Glory, he'll get down on it, ere
  he stirs a peg.

There we leave him standing,
  shouting for all hands,
Whilst all around him every
  drinker stands:
His eyes are on the keg,
  which is now lowering fast,
He works hard, he drinks
  hard, and goes to hell
  at last!

Kookaburra Sits on the Old Gum Tree

This song is widely known overseas. It is one of many songs
about Australia which is taught in schools in other countries.
For information about kookaburras, see page 186.

Kookaburra sits on the old
  gum tree,
Merry, merry king of the bush
  is he,
Laugh! kookaburra, laugh!
  kookaburra,
Gay your life must be.

Kookaburra sits on the old
  gum tree,
Eating all the gum nuts he
  can see,
Stop! kookaburra, stop!
  kookaburra,
Please leave some for me.

The Man From Snowy River

A B ('Banjo') Paterson

This dramatic story has long been a favourite among Australians. It inspired the film of the same name.

There was movement at the
station, for the word had
passed around
That the colt from old
Regret had got away,
And had joined the wild bush
horses—he was worth a
thousand pound,
So all the cracks had
gathered to the fray.
All the tried and noted riders
from the stations near
and far
Had mustered at the
homestead overnight,
For the bushmen love hard
riding where the wild bush
horses are,
And the stock-horse snuffs
the battle with delight.

There was Harrison, who
made his pile when Pardon
won the cup,
The old man with his hair as
white as snow;
But few could ride beside him
when his blood was
fairly up—
He would go wherever
horse and man could go.
And Clancy of the Overflow
came down to lend a hand,
No better horseman ever
held the reins;
For never horse could throw
him while the saddle-girths
would stand—
He learnt to ride while

droving on the plains.
And one was there, a stripling
on a small and weedy
beast;
He was something like a
racehorse undersized,
With a touch of Timor pony—
three parts thoroughbred
at least—
And such as are by
mountain horsemen prized.
He was hard and tough and
wiry—just the sort that
won't say die—
There was courage in his
quick impatient tread;
And he bore the badge of
gameness in his bright and
fiery eye,
And the proud and lofty
carriage of his head.

But still so slight and weedy;
one would doubt his power
to stay,
And the old man said, 'That
horse will never do
For a long and tiring gallop—
lad, you'd better stop away,
Those hills are far too
rough for such as you'.
So he waited, sad and
wistful—only Clancy stood
his friend—
'I think we ought to let him
come,' he said:
'I warrant he'll be with us
when he's wanted at
the end,

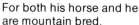

For both his horse and he
are mountain bred.
'He hails from Snowy River,
up by Kosciusko's side,
Where the hills are twice as
steep and twice as rough;
Where a horse's hoofs strike
firelight from the flint stones
every stride,
The man that holds his own
is good enough.
And the Snowy River riders
on the mountains make
their home,
Where the river runs those
giant hills between;
I have seen full many
horsemen since I first
commenced to roam,
But nowhere yet such
horsemen have I seen.'

So he went; they found the
horses by the big mimosa
clump,
They raced away towards
the mountain's brow,
And the old man gave his
orders, 'Boys, go at them
from the jump,
No use to try for fancy
riding now,
And, Clancy, you must wheel
them, try and wheel them to
the right.
Ride boldly, lad, and never
fear the spills,
For never yet was rider that
could keep the mob
in sight,
If once they gain the shelter
of those hills'.

So Clancy rode to wheel

them—he was racing
on the wing
Where the best and boldest
riders take their place,
And he raced his stock-horse
past them, and he made the
ranges ring
With the stockwhip, as he
met them face to face.
Then they halted for a
moment, while he swung
the dreaded lash,
But they saw their well-
loved mountain full in view,
And they charged beneath
the stockwhip with a sharp
and sudden dash,
And off into the mountain
scrub they flew.

Then fast the horsemen
followed, where the gorges
deep and black
Resounded to the thunder
of their tread,
And the stockwhips woke the
echoes, and they fiercely
answered back
From cliffs and crags that
beetled overhead.
And upward, ever upward, the
wild horses held their way,
Where mountain ash and
kurrajong grew wide;
And the old man muttered
fiercely, 'We may bid the
mob good day,
No man can hold them
down the other side'.

When they reached the
mountain's summit, even
Clancy took a pull—
It well might make the

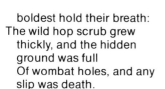

boldest hold their breath:
The wild hop scrub grew
thickly, and the hidden
ground was full
Of wombat holes, and any
slip was death.
But the man from Snowy
River let the pony have
his head,
And he swung his
stockwhip round and gave
a cheer,
And he raced him down the
mountain like a torrent
down its bed,
While the others stood and
watched in very fear.

He sent the flint-stones flying,
but the pony kept his feet,
He cleared the fallen timber
in his stride,
And the man from Snowy
River never shifted
in his seat—
It was grand to see that
mountain horseman ride.
Through the stringy barks and
saplings, on the rough and
broken ground,
Down the hillside at a
racing pace he went;
And he never drew the bridle
till he landed safe
and sound
At the bottom of that
terrible descent.

He was right among the
horses as they climbed the
farther hill,
And the watchers on the
mountain, standing mute,
Saw him ply the stockwhip

fiercely; he was right
among them still
As he raced across the
clearing in pursuit.
Then they lost him for a
moment, where two
mountain gullies met
In the ranges—but a final
glimpse reveals
On a dim and distant hillside
the wild horses racing yet,
With the man from Snowy
River at their heels.

And he ran them single-
handed till their sides were
white with foam
He followed like a
bloodhound on their track,
Till they halted, cowed and
beaten; then he turned their
heads for home,
And alone and unassisted
brought them back.
But his hardy mountain pony
he could scarcely raise a
trot,
He was blood from hip to
shoulder from the spur;
But his pluck was still
undaunted, and his
courage fiery hot,
For never yet was mountain
horse a cur.

And down by Kosciusko,
where the pine-clad ridges
raise
Their torn and rugged
battlements on high,
Where the air is clear as
crystal, and the white stars
fairly blaze
At midnight in the cold and

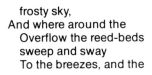

frosty sky,
And where around the
  Overflow the reed-beds
  sweep and sway
  To the breezes, and the

rolling plains are wide,
The Man from Snowy River is
  a household word today,
  And the stockmen tell the
  story of his ride.

Ballad of the Drover

Henry Lawson

Lawson is one of Australia's best loved writers. His vivid descriptions of the self-reliant bush folk of the turn of the century, are legendary. His poems depict the 'hard time,' endured by people employed in the pastoral industry and praise the courage with which they faced adversity. There is a gentle humour which sets his work apart, while his sympathy for the 'common man' reflects the feeling of 'mateship' which is familiar to most Australians.

Across the stony ridges,
  Across the rolling plain,
Young Harry Dale, the drover,
  Comes riding home again.
And well his stock-horse
    bears him,
  And light of heart is he,
And stoutly his old packhorse
  Is trotting by his knee.

Up Queensland way with
    cattle
  He's travelled regions vast,
And many months have
    vanished
  Since home-folks saw him
    last.
He hums a song of someone
  He hopes to marry soon;
And hobble-chains and camp-
    ware
  Keep jingling to the tune.

An hour has filled the heavens
  With storm-clouds inky
    black;
At times the lightning trickles
  Around the drover's track;

But Harry pushes onward,
  His horses' strength he
    tries,
In hope to reach the river
  Before the flood shall rise.

When flashes next the
    lightning,
  The flood's grey breast is
    blank;
A cattle-dog and packhorse
  Are struggling up the bank,
But in the lonely homestead
  The girl shall wait in vain —
He'll never pass the stations
  In charge of stock again.

Across the flooded lowlands
  And slopes of sodden loam
The packhorse struggles
    bravely
  To take dumb tidings home;
And mud-stained, wet, and
    weary,
  He goes by rock and tree,
With clanging chains and
    tinware
  All sounding eerily.

My Country

Dorothea Mackellar

This song of praise, written in 1908, became one of Australia's best known and loved poems. The young poet was fiercely proud of her colonial upbringing even though others felt that the bonds of loyalty to England should be strong and unquestioned. This poem reflects the intensity of her own love for her country.

The love of field and coppice,
Of green and shaded lanes,
Of ordered woods and
   gardens
Is running in your veins;
Strong love of grey-blue
   distance,
Brown streams and soft,
   dim skies—
I know, but cannot share it,
My love is otherwise.

I love a sunburnt country,
A land of sweeping plains,
Of ragged mountain ranges,
Of droughts and flooding
   rains;
I love her far horizons,
I love her jewel-sea,
Her beauty and her terror—
The wide brown land for me!

The stark white ring-barked
   forests,
All tragic to the moon,
The sapphire-misted
   mountains,
The hot gold hush of noon,
Green tangle of the brushes
Where lithe lianas coil,
And orchids deck the
   tree-tops,

And ferns the warm dark soil.

Core of my heart, my country!
Her pitiless blue sky,
When, sick at heart,
   around us
We see the cattle die—
But then the grey clouds
   gather,
And we can bless again
The drumming of an army,
The steady soaking rain.

Core of my heart, my country!
Land of the rainbow gold,
For flood and fire and famine
She pays us back threefold.
Over the thirsty paddocks,
Watch, after many days,
The filmy veil of greenness
That thickens as we gaze . . .

An opal-hearted country,
A wilful, lavish land—
All you who have not
   loved her,
You will not understand—
Though Earth holds many
   splendours,
Wherever I may die,
I know to what brown country
My homing thoughts will fly.

The Man From Ironbark

A B ('Banjo') Paterson

As sophistication developed among city dwellers, at the end of the 19th century, there was a growing tendency to regard the bushman as a rural clown. This is a whimsical glimpse of the way one such 'clown' dealt with the situation.

tote   — a record and distribution of a bet
yokel   — a country bumpkin
peeler   — a policeman

It was the man from Ironbark who struck the Sydney town,
He wandered over street and park, he wandered up and down.
He loitered here, he loitered there, till he was like to drop,
Until at last in sheer despair he sought a barber's shop.
' 'Ere! shave my beard and whiskers off, I'll be a man of mark,
I'll go and do the Sydney toff up home in Ironbark.'

The barber man was small and flash, as barbers mostly are,
He wore a strike-your-fancy sash, he smoked a huge cigar:
He was a humorist of note and keen at repartee,
He laid the odds and kept a 'tote', whatever that may be.
And when he saw our friend arrive, he whispered 'Here's a lark!
Just watch me catch him all alive this man from Ironbark'.

There were some gilded youths that sat along the barber's wall,
Their eyes were dull, their heads were flat, they had no brains at all;
To them the barber passed the wink, his dexter eyelid shut,
'I'll make this bloomin' yokel think his bloomin' throat is cut'.
And as he soaped and rubbed it in he made a rude remark.
'I s'pose the flats is pretty green up there in Ironbark.'

A grunt was all reply he got; he shaved the bushman's chin,
Then made the water boiling hot and dipped the razor in.
He raised his hand, his brow grew black, he paused a while to gloat,
Then slashed the red-hot razor-back across his victim's throat;
Upon the newly shaven chin it made a livid mark—
No doubt it fairly took him in—the man from Ironbark.

He fetched a wild up-country

yell might wake the dead
to hear,
And though his throat, he
knew full well, was cut from
ear to ear,
He struggled gamely to his
feet, and faced the
murderous foe.
'You've done for me! you dog,
I'm beat! one hit
before I go!
I only wish I had a knife, you
blessed murdering shark!
But you'll remember all your
life the man from Ironbark.'

He lifted up his hairy paw,
with one tremendous clout
And landed on the barber's
jaw, and knocked the
barber out.
He set to work with tooth and
nail, he made the place a
wreck;
He grabbed the nearest
gilded youth, and tried to
break his neck.
And all the while his throat he
held to save his vital spark,
And 'Murder! Bloody Murder!'
yelled the man from
Ironbark.

A peeler man who heard the
din came in to
see the show!
He tried to run the bushman
in, but he refused to go.
And when at last the barber
spoke, and said ' 'Twas all
in fun—
'Twas just a harmless little
joke, a trifle overdone'.
'A joke!' he cried, 'By George,
that's fine; a lively sort of
lark;
I'd like to catch that
murdering swine some
night in Ironbark'.

And now while round the
shearing-floor the listening
shearers gape,
He tells the story o'er and
o'er, and brags of his
escape.
'Them barber chaps what
keeps a tote, by George,
I've had enough,
One tried to cut my bloomin'
throat, but thank the Lord
it's tough.'
And whether he's believed or
no, there's one thing to
remark,
That flowing beards are all the
go way up in Ironbark.

Platypuses, plants, parrots

For millions of years the fauna of Australia evolved in isolation and many different forms came from relatively few ancestral types. As a result, Australia has some of nature's strangest creatures, which draw enthusiastic zoologists and tourists to our country to study them at first hand.

Mammals

Australia has about 230 species of mammals and almost half are marsupials, the pouched mammal. The balance consists of placental mammals (having a placenta which nourishes the embryo), and the monotremes, the lowest order of egg-laying mammals (having one opening for digestive, urinary and genital organs).

Marsupials

Most of the world's marsupials are found in Australia.

Bandicoot

This small rat-like marsupial of the Peramelidae family is interesting because of its zoological likeness to the kangaroo and possum families and yet it is insectivorous (insect eating) and resembles the flesh-eating native cat. Bandicoots are found in most parts of Australia.

Koala

Phascolarctos cinereus

This enchanting little animal is unique to Australia. It is not a member of the bear family, but a marsupial; it has a pouch which opens downwards. The koala is a tree dweller, drowsing during the daytime and becoming more active in the evening, and feeding on vast quantities of gum leaves which have a high oil content. This enables them to go without water for long periods of time. The koala is Queensland's animal emblem.

Kangaroos

Kangaroos are represented in Australia by three sub-families. The most primitive is the rat-kangaroo, Hypsiprymnodontinae, which is thought to be the connecting link between the possum and kangaroo families. The second sub-family, the Potoroinae, is represented by the more advanced typical rat-kangaroo, and the third and most varied sub-family, the Macropodinae embraces the most advanced herbivorous (plant-eating) kind. This includes small scrub and rock wallabies, the large or brush wallaby and the typical large kangaroos.

The kangaroo is a marsupial whose pouch opens upwards unlike the koala's. It has a unique continuous flow of reproduction, with one joey outside the pouch which will still suckle, one inside suckling, and one embryo 'on hold'. Thus the female can produce offspring long after the male has disappeared. They are also capable of limiting reproduction during drought.

There are 45 species of kangaroo in Australia. They are bipedal (two-footed) having a remarkable hopping action which prevents them from easily moving backwards. The kangaroo represents the world's only marsupial group to become entirely dependent on this specialised form of locomotion. The kangaroo is Australia's unofficial animal emblem.

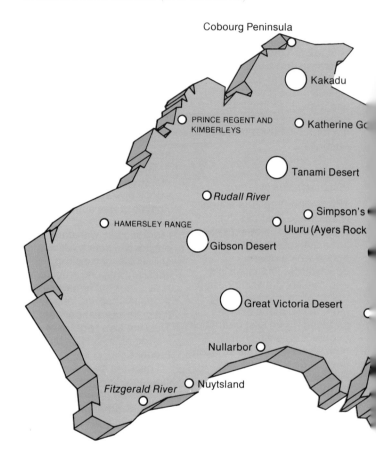

Cobourg Peninsula

Kakadu

PRINCE REGENT AND
KIMBERLEYS

Katherine Go

Tanami Desert

Rudall River

Simpson's

HAMERSLEY RANGE

Uluru (Ayers Rock

Gibson Desert

Great Victoria Desert

Nullarbor

Fitzgerald River Nuytsland

Sou

The 'Queensland' tree kangaroo, *Dendrolagus lumholtzi*, is a unique animal which lives in the trees of the rainforests. It has evolved because of pressure on the ground food supplies. Over millions of years it has undergone a reversal of development, returning to the tree haunts of its primitive possum-like ancestors.

The red kangaroo, *Macropus rufus*, and the great grey kangaroo, *Macropus giganteus*, are the largest marsupials. A height of 2.92 metres and a weight of more than 100 kilograms has been recorded. The red kangaroo is the Northern Territory's animal emblem.

The musk rat-kangaroo, *Hypsiprymnodon moschatus*, is the smallest of the kangaroos and lives in the Atherton Tableland of the north coast of Queensland. It is less than 300 millimetres long.

Marsupial mole

Notoryctes typhlops

This small animal lives in desert regions of southern and western Australia. It is eyeless and has no claws, unlike the true mole. It tunnels with its fleshy feet through loose sand and is rarely found because it stays underground.

175

Numbat
Myrmecobius fasciatus

This unique striped marsupial is found only in Western Australia. It is considered to be an endangered species as it is widely hunted by feral animals. It has sharp front claws and a sticky tongue with which it attacks ant and termite nests. However, it can open only the weakest nest and is unable to completely destroy it as it can't burrow too far in. Although it is a marsupial, strangely it has no pouch. Instead the young (usually four), cling with their mouths to the mother's underside until old enough to fend for themselves. The numbat is Western Australia's animal emblem.

Possums

Australian possums, or phalangers, are herbivorous marsupials which live in trees. They belong to four main families: ringtails and large gliders; brushtails and cuscus; feathertail and pygmy possums and honey possums. They are shy nocturnal creatures. Some are capable of gliding but it is not considered true flight. They have a pouch but also carry their young on their backs.

The greater glider possum, *Petauroides volans*, is an elusive creature which usually finds a home in the hollow of a gum tree. It is capable of gliding or volplaning from one tree to another by an extension of skin along the sides of the body and limbs, which when extended forms a sort of parachute.

Leadbeater's possum, *Gymaobelideus leadbeateri*, is a tiny possum which lives only in Victoria over an area of 100 square kilometres extending from Marysville, north-west of Melbourne, to Tanjil Bren. After 1909 it was thought to be extinct but was re-discovered in 1961, again at Marysville. It is the animal emblem of Victoria.

Tasmanian devil
Sarcophilus harrisii

The Tasmanian devil is the largest surviving carnivorous (meat-eating) marsupial. It is nocturnal and very shy, belying its name. It is the size of a fox terrier but has strength enough in its teeth to consume a whole sheep, including the skull. Usually there are litters of four which remain in the pouch for several months.

DID YOU KNOW?

The mature Karri tree of Western Australia can yield more than 250 kilograms of honey from its estimated 500 000 blossoms.

Tasmanian devil

Tasmanian tiger
Thylacinus cynocephalus

Also known as the thylacine, this is the largest carnivorous marsupial in the world. It is presumed extinct, although there are many unconfirmed sightings. Thylacines were at one time very common but a bounty placed upon them caused widespread destruction. The last one was caught in 1933 and died in Melbourne in 1936. They are wolf-like but are not related to the canine family. As a rule the litter numbers four, the young remaining in the pouch for perhaps three months before they are ready to leave the 'nursery'.

Wombats

The wombat is a powerful, thickset burrowing marsupial found only in Australia. The common wombat, *Vombatus ursinus*, is a forest dweller and the hairy-nosed wombat, *latifrons* and *Lasiorhinus krefftii* are plains dwellers. Because of loss of habitat, the northern *L. krefftii* is considered an endangered species. It is not a very sociable animal. The wombat has a bony plate in its rump, which can be used to kill any predator which might follow the wombat down its burrow by crushing it against the roof of the burrow. Because of their instinct to go through things rather than go around, wombats are often considered stupid and destructive. However, they have a brain proportionally larger than any other marsupial, indicating high intelligence. The hairy-nosed wombat is South

Australia's animal emblem.

Placental mammals

Australia's placental mammals comprise bats, the dingo, marine mammals and rodents. Placental mammals produce fully developed young.

Bats

Bats are the only true flying mammal. They are warm-blooded and are covered in fur. They nourish their young with milk. They can fly long distances, using echo location to find their way. As a result they have a highly developed sense of smell and hearing. The order bats are represented in Australia by fifty-eight species including the fruit bats, *Chiroptera pteropodidae*, as well as the rare ghost bat, *Macroderma gigas*, of central Australia, which is a cannibal bat, living on smaller species of its own kind and other animals.

Dingo

Canis familiaris dingo

This dog is regarded as indigenous to Australia, and is presumed to have evolved from dogs brought from Asia 3000 to 8000 years ago by the

Dingo

ancestors of the Australian Aboriginal. They are stealthy nocturnal hunters and often set up a continual chorus of dismal howls, much like the northern hemisphere wolf.

Marine mammals

Sea lions, of the family Otariidae, and seals, of the family Phocidae, are ocean mammals which are found on Australia's southern coastline. Seals have limited mobility on land as they have to drag their hind limbs; sea lions, with more use of their hind limbs, are more mobile.

Dugongs, *Dugong dugon*, are completely herbivorous. They graze on the sea grasses on the ocean bottom as sheep graze in a paddock.

Rodents

There are numerous species of native Australian rodents. They are not as prolific in breeding habits as introduced species so they are not as widespread, nor are they considered a pest.

Monotremes

Echidna

Tachyglossus aculeatus

These bizarre creatures, together with the platypus, are the world's only egg-laying mammals. The echidna, or spiny ant-eater, has sharp claws and a long sticky ribbon-like tongue with which it gathers up ants and termites at lightning speed. It has no teeth, and relies on its stiff spines for protection. It lays a single egg which is carried and hatched in a temporary but commodious pouch formed from folds of skin. The female has no teats. The milk is exuded into the pouch and is licked up by the baby.

Platypus

Ornithorhynchus anatinus

This animal, unique to Australia, is the world's strangest aquatic mammal. It has often been considered a living fossil and may be the missing link between reptiles and mammals. It has webbed clawed feet and a duck-like bill, which is fleshy and sensitive, for foraging food. It has beaver-like fur and tail, lays eggs and suckles its young, and just to make things more complicated, the male has a poison spur behind its back leg, the reason for which is not known. It inhabits the eastern watercourses, making its burrow entrance above the

---

DID YOU KNOW?

Because of its suitability to immersion in water, timber from the Satinay tree was shipped to Egypt from Fraser Island in 1925, to prop up the walls of the Suez Canal.

water-line. The platypus is the animal emblem of New South Wales.

Introduced species

Australia has many introduced species of mammal, which have gone wild (feral). These include the rabbit, hare, horse, donkey, deer, camel, fox, pig, goat, sheep, cow, rat, mouse, dog, cat and water buffalo. Some are regarded as pests and cause considerable damage to agriculture and to native plants and animals.

Reptiles and amphibians

Australia has about 140 species of snake, 360 species of lizard, two species of crocodile, fifteen species of freshwater tortoise and six species of marine turtle.

Crocodiles

Both species of Australian crocodiles are found in our northern waters. The freshwater crocodile, *Crocodylus johnstoni*, is not dangerous to people; however, the saltwater species, *C. porosus*, which can grow to 7 metres long, is dangerous. Both are protected, as it is felt that they are endangered. Not only are they hunted for their skins, but it is believed low-flying aircraft disturb the females, so that they leave their eggs unprotected to be eaten by predators.

Frogs

There are approximately 130 species of frog in Australia, but no salamanders.
Australia's native frogs include a diverse array of tree frogs, marsh frogs and burrowing frogs.

The golden swamp frog, from the genus *Limnodynastes*, is the most widely distributed frog in Australia.

The gastric brooding frog, *Rheobatrachusilus*, was first discovered in 1973. It is unique in the animal world because the female inhibits its gastric juices and turns its stomach into a uterus. It swallows the fertile eggs, which turn into fully developed young in the temporary nursery. The young then emerge through the mouth.

The water-holding frog of Australia, *Cyclorana platycephalus*, appears above ground only after rain. As it is a desert creature it has long spells in its cocoon-like chamber below ground. During wet times, it fills the chamber with water and then sits in the water till the drought is over.

The corroboree frog, *Pseudophryne corroboree*,

grows to 3 centimetres long and is pale green with black markings.

The cane toad, *Bufo marinus*, of South America was introduced into Australia in 1935 to control cane-borer beetles. It failed to do this but since then it has spread in plague proportions along the east coast.

Lizards

Australian lizards range in size from 55 millimetres to 2.4 metres long. Our great perentie or goanna, *Varanus giganteus*, is the second-largest lizard in the world.

Our most popular lizard is the frill-necked lizard, *Chlamydosaurus kingii*. It has a vivid frill of skin which is normally folded back. Under attack, it unfolds the frill, sways to and fro, opens its mouth wide and hisses. However, it does not readily attack, and if in doubt, runs at great speed on its back legs. (In other words it knows when to quit!)

The blue-tongue lizard of which *Tiliqua scincoides* is the most common, belongs to the skink family of lizards. They are the most prevalent in Australia.

The moloch or thorny devil, *Moloch horridus*, is well protected from predators by its ability to camouflage itself. It also has skin armour so

sharp that no animal could eat it without injuring itself.

Snakes

Only about 140 species of snake are found in Australia and of these, approximately 100 are venomous. The non-venomous snakes include pythons, blind snakes, file snakes and some colubrid snakes. The largest is the amethystine or scrub python, *Morelia Liasis amethystina*, which grows to about 7 metres and the smallest are the carpet python, *Morelia spilota variegata*, and diamond python, *Morelia spilota spilotes*, both of which reach a length of 2-4 metres.

Among the venomous snakes are the death adder, *Acanthopis*. It grows to a length of about 60 centimetres, and its venom is more potent than that of the Indian Cobra. It has a broad flat constricted head, and a short thin tail.

The tiger snake of the genus *Notechis* is distributed throughout the southern part of the continent. This aggressive and dangerous snake does not grow more than 2 metres in length. The venom is more powerful than that of any other land snake. It is coloured from tan to olive with dark bands across the body.

The 3.4 metre taipan, *Oxyuranus scutellatus*, of

Queensland is one of the world's most venomous land snakes. It carries enough venom to kill 23 000 mice. It is brown and is our largest venomous species.

There are over thirty species of sea snakes found in our northern waters, the most common of which is the yellow-bellied sea snake, *Pelamis platurus*.

Earthworms

The world's largest earthworm, *Megascolides australis*, is found in Gippsland in Victoria. It grows to 3.56 metres long and 1.9 centimetres in diameter.

Insects

Australia has over 50 000 species of insect. There are about 350 species of butterfly, 7600 species of moth, 18 000 species of beetle and 900 species of ant.

Cicadas

There are over 200 species of Australian cicada, having such fanciful names as double drummer, *Thopha saccata*, cherry nose,

Macrtristria angularis, red eye, *Psaltoda moerens*, black prince, *P. plaga*, and yellow Monday and green Monday (or greengrocer), *Cyclochila australasiae*. The nymphs (the young) live beneath the ground for several years before hatching, living on sap tapped from the roots of trees. They finally emerge and within weeks they mate and die.

It is only the male cicada which sings so deafeningly. A collection of them can produce a noise in excess of 120 decibels, equal to the noise produced by a very loud rock band.

Arachnids

The funnel-web spider, *Atrax robustus*, is the most poisonous spider in Australia. The male is five times more toxic than the female. It is found only in a small area of coastal New South Wales.

The male red-back spider, *Latrodectus mactans*, is one-third the size of the female and is reputed to be non-poisonous. The female, on the other hand, is highly venomous.

DID YOU KNOW?
Sharks have caused more deaths in Australia than anywhere else. Even so, since 1791, fewer than a hundred people have been killed.

Australia's magnetic termite, *Amitermes meridionalis*, builds a nest approximately 4 metres high, 3 metres long and 1 metre wide. The narrow ends point north-south, and so the nest is called a meridional or compass nest. They have been used as direction finders by lost travellers.

Marine organisms

The Great Barrier Reef

The Great Barrier Reef, the largest and most intricate expanse of coral reefs in the world, extends along the Queensland coast for more than 2000 kilometres, covering a total area of almost 260 000 square kilometres.

The earth's largest structure created by living creatures, this reef began forming more than 10 000 years ago. It is a complex ecological maze of fortress-like structures composed of dead coral, over which the living coral forms a mantle. The living coral, made up of millions of coral polyps, produces a limestone secretion for support and protection. These tiny marine animals, whose growth and reproduction build on to the remains of their ancestors, in turn create a still larger and more complex coral colony.

Between the outer Barrier Reef and the coast, ridges of small reefs have developed. Here corals of brilliant colours and fantastic designs live in the sheltered waters: mushroom coral; brain-like coral with intricate cerebral engravings; organ-pipe and gorgonian corals; delicate traceries of lace in the shapes of fans and ferns. There are 'table-tops' and many-pointed antlers and sturdy stag-horn branches. Brightly hued fish dart about the coral, clams open to display their velvet-soft linings of many hues, and anemones, with decoy fish cradled in their tentacles, feed on anything that comes within reach.

Blue-ringed octopus
Hapalochlaena maculosa

These small octopuses are found over vast areas, from inter-tidal waters to about 40 to 50 metres deep. Often they take the colour of their background, but when irritated they light up electric-blue rings around their body. Normally they are not aggressive, although if they are handled and they sting, the sting can prove fatal. The first recorded death was in 1956. The body is about the size of a 20-cent piece and the tentacles are 7 to 8 centimetres long. They can live up to one year.

In the north-west corner of the continent, a slightly larger version of the species occurs, *H. lunulosa*. It has not been proved yet whether the sting is poisonous.

Crown-of-thorns starfish
Acanthaster planci

This starfish, approximately 30 centimetres in diameter, is widespread in the Pacific region. It is not deadly, but because the spines are quite toxic it is hard to handle. In recent years, abnormal growth in numbers has occurred, not only in Australian coral reefs, but as far afield as East Africa to Guam, giving rise to the belief that the increase is more a result of natural phenomena than the result of pollutants in our seas. The starfish attacks only living coral, and there is a widely held opinion that, because the reefs mainly comprise dead coral, the relatively small amounts of living coral destroyed are no great threat to the vastness of the reef. Layers of spines of the starfish have been found in calcified coral set down over hundreds of years, indicating, perhaps, that

outbreaks may come in cycles.

Sea wasp
Chironex fleckeri

This creature is found in Australian tropical waters during summer months. It is often referred to as the box jellyfish because of its cubic shape. Roughly the size of a wine cask, it has a simple branched tentacle, flowing from each corner of the cube, which is extremely dangerous. In fact, it is considered to be the most poisonous creature in our seas. A sting can cause death within minutes. Radio warnings are given when sea wasps are sighted, and intending swimmers are well advised to change their plans.

Birds

Australia is richer in birdlife than most other countries. There are over seven hundred different kinds including the bower-builders, the lyrebirds, magpies, butcherbirds and song larks.

Bell-bird
Manorina melanophrys

Bell-birds are found in open

DID YOU KNOW?
No part of Australia is further than 1000 kilometres from the sea.

forests and sheltered dells on the eastern coast. They have a loud bell-like note and can often be heard when one is travelling around sharp bends in a road where the bushland drops away into a gully. In contrast to their beautiful song they are small and nondescript.

Black swan
Cygnus atratus

The black swan is unique to Australia and is the only species of swan on the continent. It is distributed throughout the country, building a nest, about a metre in diameter, among reeds in swamps and feeding on aquatic plants and animals. It has a trumpet-like call. It is Western Australia's bird emblem.

Bower bird

The satin bower bird, *Ptilonorhynchus violaceus*, is found only in Australia and New Guinea. The male builds a decorated bower with a series of archways and fills the area with objects to attract the female to a mating dance. She in turn builds her nest in the trees where she lays her eggs.

Brolga
Grus rubicunda

The brolga or native companion is the only Australian crane. It is a swamp dweller, found mostly on the inland plains. Flocks of brolgas perform a stately mating dance, using their long legs to perfect the formal routine of the dance.

Emu
Dromaius novaehollandiae

The emu is the unofficial bird emblem of Australia. It is flightless and stands about 1.5 metres high and is Australia's largest bird. It is closely related to the cassowary and next in size to the ostrich. The dark-green eggs average nearly a kilogram in weight. These are hatched by the male who sits for eight weeks before the chicks appear.

Despite its name, the mallee emu wren, *Stipiturus malachurus*, is Australia's smallest bird. It gets its name because its tiny tail is similar in shape to an emu feather.

Honeyeater

The helmeted honeyeater, *Meliphaga cassidix*, is one of the rarest birds in the world. It is only found in southern Victoria, east of Port Phillip. They are the only bird species restricted to that state, although they belong to the larger group of over eighty species of honeyeater. They have a yellow crest or helmet, and a yellow tuft behind each ear with a distinctly black face. The helmeted honeyeater is the bird emblem of Victoria.

Kookaburra

Unique to Australia, these birds are the largest of the kingfishers. There are two types, the laughing jackass of the eastern states, *Dacelo gigas*, and the blue-winged kookaburra, *D. Leachii*, of the north and north-west. They breed in families, so the older offspring help raise the fledglings. They 'laugh' raucously in chorus, marking out their territory. They live on reptiles, small mammals, mice and sometimes fish. The kookaburra is the bird emblem of New South Wales. A well-known song about it is on page 164.

Lyrebird

The male lyrebirds, *Menura novae hollandiae* and *M. albertii*, have a fancy gauze-like tail giving this unique bird its name. The female is nondescript in appearance. Lyrebirds are ground feeders and build incubation mounds for nests which keep the interior at 30°C. They have a wide vocal range and are splendid mimics.

Parrot

There are more than fifty species of Australian parrot. Among them are galahs, *Cacatua roseicapilla*, sulphur-crested cockatoos, *Cacatua galerita*, rosellas, of the genus *Platycercus*, lorikeets, of the

Kookaburra

genera *Trichoglossus* and *Glossopsitta*, and budgerigars, *Melopsittacus undulatus*. They are usually found in semi-arid areas, gathered together in large flocks.

Penguin

The only penguin species residing in Australian waters is the fairy or little penguin, *Eudyptula minor*. Phillip Island, near Melbourne, is the home of the best-known colony. In summer, tourists flock to Phillip Island to watch the penguin parade, as the birds waddle back to their nests after a day's fishing.

Swift and swallow

The migratory spine-tailed swift, *Hirundapus caudacutus*, is known as the storm-bird. It is seen soaring high in the sky before and after a storm, feeding on the insects trapped in the turbulence. It rarely lands but spends much of its life in the sky.

The welcome swallow, *Hirundo neoxena* spends long hours soaring. These birds can feed their young without alighting on the nest. They hover over the fledglings and drop the food.

Wedge-tailed eagle
Aquila audax

With an average wingspan of 2.5 metres, this bird is Australia's largest raptor. It is clearly recognisable by its huge broad wings and the long wedge-shaped tail. The general colour is dark brown, with a chestnut neck. The legs are feathered right down to the feet. Its hooked beak and strong talons clearly mark the wedge-tailed eagle as a bird of prey. It is found throughout Australia, and is more common in the arid centre than on coastal plains. It is the Northern Territory's bird emblem.

Plants

Although Australia is predominantly arid, with vast desert areas, there are many other vegetation regions such as rainforests, savanna grasslands, scrub, mallee, heath and alpine areas.

Australian plants in general are characterised by their drought-resistant qualities. They have tough spiny leaves and thick bark to resist evaporation. They are also very fire-resistant and indeed most of our plants need a fierce fire to germinate seeds and rejuvenate.

The Australian land flora comprises over 12 000 species of flowering plant and is dominated by *Eucalyptus* (over 550 recognised species), *Melaleuca Leptospermum* (tea-tree), *collistemon* (bottlebrush),

Banksia (honeysuckle), *Acacia* (wattle), *Casuarina* (she-oak) and *Xanthorrhoea* (blackboy). The eucalypt is the most dominant tree in Australia, and has tough, durable wood. It is able to resist the ravages of fire by sending out shoots from the trunk which keep the tree alive till the branches recover. The bark, leaves and branches are constantly shed, which creates fuel for a bushfire. As well, eucalyptus oil is highly flammable. During a bushfire, the oil creates a gas which forms fireballs. This is nature's way of keeping the fire alive so as to burn and then rejuvenate the Australian bush.

The Ku-Ring-Gai National Park, north of Sydney, was named after the Gurringai Aboriginal tribe who had lived there over 20 000 years before white settlement. It is one of the oldest national parks in Australia and contains more species of plants than are found in the whole of Great Britain. The park is 14 656 hectares.

Forests

On the northern and eastern coastlines of the Australian continent are vast areas of forest which experience rainfall ranging from 1000 to 2500 millimetres per year.

In the broad-leaved rainforests of the north buttressing fig trees, interlacing lianas, cabbage fan palms, *Livistona australis*, entanglements of lawyer vines, *Smilax australis*, eucalypts, nettle trees of the family *Urticaceae*, and fungi predominate to create a dank brooding atmosphere.

The open forests around the top end of the Northern Territory and on the east coast are less formidable and dense. Here eucalypts such as mountain ash, *E. regnans*, spotted gum, *E. maculata* and hoop pine, *Araucaria cunninghamii*, dominate the landscape, with the perennial plants, like prickly Moses, *Acacia ulicifolia*, and purple coral-pea, *Hardenbergia violacea*, flowering in spring. In the New South Wales and Tasmanian forests the waratah, *Telopea speciosissima*, blooms with its crimson composite flower, 10 centimetres wide, on a single straight stem. The waratah is the floral emblem of New South Wales.

Golden wattle, *Acacia pycnantha*, is Australia's unofficial floral emblem. It is one of 850 species of Australian acacia also found in scrublands. The bark is a source of gum arabic used in tanning. Wattle has fragrant golden yellow flowers.

The common pink heath,

Epacris impressa labill, is Victoria's floral emblem. It occurs mainly in the southern part of Victoria, chiefly in the wetter foothill country, the coastal heathlands, the Grampians and the Little Desert scrub. It grows to about 1200 metres above sea level.

The Cooktown orchid, *Dendrobium bigibbum,* is native to tropical Queensland, and has been chosen as the floral emblem of that state. It has purple flowers about 4 centimetres across; the orchid grows in rocks and trees in well-watered areas of Cape York Peninsula.

Grasses and woodlands

These areas of Australia are to be found mainly 200 to 300 kilometres inland from the north and eastern coast. There is a greater distance between the trees than in the forests and the tree crowns are quite large. Here the eucalypt abounds and varieties such as yellow box, *E. melliodora*, white cypress pine, *Callitris columellaris*, Darwin stringybark, *E. tetrodonta*, and river red gum, *E. camaldulensis*, flower in spring and summer.

The gradual blending of woodland into grassland produces a more sporadic grouping of trees intermingled with varieties of grasses such as kangaroo grass, *Themeda australis*, and blue devil, *Eryngium rostratum*.

An unusual plant of the grasslands is the subterranean orchid, *Rhizanthella gardneri*. It is found in the wheat-belt of south-east Western Australia. It exists wholly beneath the soil and does not disturb the surface. Farmers found this elusive plant while ploughing. It is thought that it could become extinct because of loss of natural habitat.

Scrub and mallee

This is a diverse community of shrubby plants where the most dominant, the Mallee eucalyptus, is no more than 8 metres high. It is restricted to the south-eastern and south-western regions of the country where many Australian wild flowers grow. The saw banksia, *Banksia serrata*, grows in this area. It was named after Sir Joseph Banks, the botanist who came with Captain Cook on the

---

DID YOU KNOW?
Mt Kosciusko, 2228 metres above sea level, is Australia's highest peak.

Endeavour.

Banksia species (bottle-brushes) are considered to be the honeysuckle trees of Australia. Like most Australian plants they need an extremely hot fire to germinate their seeds. May Gibbs, the Australian author of children's books, immortalised this tree by creating the Bad Banksia Men characters in *Snugglepot and Cuddlepie*.

Deserts

The true desert prevails over vast regions of the inland. Here the land receives unpredictable and extremely low rainfall, temperatures are extreme, and the evaporation exceeds precipitation. These adverse conditions not only create a variety of dry salt lakes and dry riverbeds but produce a complex mosaic of plant communities. Plants adapt by growing spindly leaves and tough bark to stop evaporation in the extreme heat. Again the eucalypts, coolabah, *E. microtheca*, and ghost gum, *E. papuana*, dominate the desert trees. The unusual bottle trees, for example *Brachychiton rupestre*, derive their name from their bottle-shaped trunk. The branches look like the roots of the tree, which resulted in an Aboriginal myth that the tree lives upside down. It has adapted well to desert conditions by storing water in its trunk.

Porcupine grass, such as *Triodia irritans*, and saltbush, *Atriplex vesicaria*, are the dominant plants in Australian desert areas. They are tough grasses of rounded tussocks and sharp pointed leaves. Being drought-resistant, the seeds are dispersed by the dried plant tumbling in the wind.

Sturt's desert rose, *Gossypium sturtianum*, is a small bushy plant, growing to a height of 1.5 metres, with dark green leaves. The petals of the flowers are mauve, with deep red markings at the base. Sturt's desert rose is an arid-zone plant and is found in the southern part of the Northern Territory and was adopted·for its emblem in 1974. It was named for Captain Charles Sturt, an explorer, see p 10.

Sturt's desert pea, *Clianthus formosus*, is South Australia's floral emblem. It is a creeper with brilliant scarlet and black flowers, growing only in dry, sandy country.

DID YOU KNOW?
Fifty per cent of the continent has less than 300 millimetres annual rainfall.

Palate: dinky-di recipes

In the early days of the colony the precarious food supplies resulted in a staple diet of meat and cheese tempered with some vegetables and wheat products. It was mainly based on English fare and by 1900, regardless of our long hot summers, the preference for hot meals with plenty of meat still persisted. In fact, Australians were recognised as the greatest meat eaters in the world. Even the middle class rarely ate fresh fruit or salads and our wonderful variety of sea-food was largely unrecognised.

There was little change in our dietary habits until the post-war immigration years when the introduction of cuisines from many lands widened our culinary horizons.

While there is now a more cosmopolitan attitude to the selection of food, Australians still retain from the early days many traditional recipes which have always remained popular.

Lamingtons

These small cakes were popularised by Queenslanders in the early 1900s.

¾ cup butter
¾ cup castor sugar
½ teaspoon vanilla
3 eggs
1 cup self-raising flour
½ cup plain flour
½ cup milk
chocolate icing and desiccated coconut

Beat butter and sugar until creamy. Add 2 eggs, one at a time and beat well.

Add the vanilla and half the sifted flour and baking powder. Mix well. Add milk and remaining flour and the third egg and mix until smooth.

Place in a well-greased lamington tin (or baking-dish) and bake for 30 minutes in a moderate to slow oven. Cool and cut into small squares.

Spear each square on a carving fork, dip in chocolate icing, drain, toss in desiccated coconut.

Famous cornflour sponge cake

A Royal Show special.

3 eggs separated
pinch of salt
¼ teaspoon vanilla
½ cup castor sugar
⅔ cup cornflour
1 slightly rounded tablespoon plain flour
1 level teaspoon baking powder

Pre-heat oven to 190°C (or 375°F). Beat egg whites with salt until soft peaks form. Gradually beat in sugar, a little at a time, then continue beating until stiff.

Add egg yolks and vanilla. Beat until combined. Sift together three times the cornflour, plain flour and baking powder. Add to egg mixture. Carefully and lightly fold into mixture with wooden spoon. Do not stir.

Divide batter evenly between two greased and lightly floured 20 centimetre round sandwich pans. Bake 18–20 minutes.

Pumpkin scones

These moist delicious scones are old favourites.

1 level tablespoon butter
3 level tablespoons sugar
¾ cup cooked mashed pumpkin
1 egg
2 cups self-raising flour
pinch salt
¼ cup milk

Cream the butter and sugar, add the egg and mix. Fold in the pumpkin.

Sift the flour and fold in with beaten egg and milk.

Knead well. Roll out the dough and cut with a scone-cutter into circles. Bake in a hot oven for 15 minutes.

Queensland Blue pumpkin soup

The Queensland Blue is a variety of pumpkin which is noted for its flavour and keeping qualities. The quantities given will serve six people.

¾ cup butter
4½ cups peeled chopped pumpkin
½ cup chopped onion
2 cups water
3 tablespoons plain flour
1 cup milk
1 egg

Melt ½ cup butter in heavy pan, add pumpkin and onion. Cook for 10 minutes with the lid on, stirring occasionally. Add water and simmer until the pumpkin is very tender.

Press through a sieve or puree in a blender with a little of the milk.

Melt the rest of the butter and stir in the flour. Gradually add the puree of pumpkin and the remaining milk, stirring constantly. Simmer for 20 minutes.

Just before serving combine egg yolk with a little of pumpkin mixture, then stir into pumpkin soup.

Billy tea

To be had where old mates yarn.

Place a billycan of fresh stream water onto hot coals of a fire. When it is boiling, sprinkle in a handful of tea leaves and allow to boil one minute. Drop in a green gum leaf or two for flavour. Allow the brew to stand by the fire for two minutes. Tap sides with stick to settle the tea leaves and pour tea into mugs. Some old-timers 'swing the billy' of boiling tea around their heads. This is a sure way of making a good brew.

Peach Melba

This dessert was named for the famous singer, Dame Nellie Melba.

3 large peaches
vanilla ice-cream
whipped cream
raspberry syrup

Cook the peaches carefully so they do not break. Drain, cut in half and chill. Place cut side up in individual dishes. Fill each with a scoop of ice-cream, and top with whipped cream. Pour raspberry syrup around peaches.

Pavlova

The Pavlova was created in 1935 by chef Bert Sachse, while he was working at Perth's Esplanade Hotel. He made it in honour of the hotel's most distinguished guest of previous years, the great prima-ballerina, Anna Matveena Pavlova. It is now considered to be a national dish.

This popular party dessert consists of a shell of meringue, filled with whipped cream and fresh fruit.

4 egg whites
pinch salt
1¼ cups castor sugar
1 teaspoon vinegar
2 teaspoons cornflour
whipped cream
fruit to decorate

Heat oven to moderate. Mark 20-centimetre circle on greaseproof paper. Brush paper with oil and place on greased oven tray.

Beat egg whites and salt on high speed until stiff but not dry. Gradually add sugar, a tablespoon at a time, beating well after each addition. Meringue should be smooth and glossy and hold firm peaks.

Remove beaters and sprinkle vinegar and cornflour over top of mixture and fold in lightly.

Spoon mixture onto the greased paper circle and spread evenly. Make a depression in the middle with back of spoon.

Place in bottom half of oven and immediately reduce heat to low. Bake 1½ hours. Turn off heat and allow to cool in the oven.

When cool, fill with whipped cream and decorate with strawberries, sliced kiwi fruit and passionfruit.

Vegemite pinwheels

These are made from the famous Kraft product Vegemite—
favourite of all Australians. The quantities given will make
about 4½ dozen.

2 cups self-raising flour
1 good pinch of cayenne pepper
1 teaspoon of dry mustard
2 tablespoons butter
1½ cups grated cheese
⅓ cup water
Vegemite

Sift the dry ingredients together. Rub in the butter and add
cheese. Mix to a firm dough with water.

Turn out onto a floured board and knead well. Roll pastry
into a rectangle. Spread with Vegemite and roll into a long coil.

Cut into pinwheel slices and place flat on greased tray. Bake
in hot oven 15–20 minutes.

Bush brownie

A stockman's stand-by.

1½ cups self-raising flour
¾ cup butter
½ cup brown sugar
2 cups mixed fruit
1 egg
1 cup milk
1 teaspoon each of ginger, all-spice, nutmeg

Sift dry ingredients in bowl. Rub in butter. Add fruit. Mix in
well-beaten egg and milk.

Pour into greased tin and bake 30–40 minutes in moderate
oven. Serve sliced and buttered.

Anzac biscuits

A crisp tasty treat with good keeping qualities. Often sent to Australian soldiers at Gallipoli by loving families. The quantities given will make about 5 dozen biscuits.

½ cup butter
1 tablespoon golden syrup
½ teaspoon bicarbonate of soda
2 tablespoons boiling water
1 cup uncooked rolled oats
1 cup desiccated coconut
1 cup plain flour
1 cup brown sugar
2 teaspoons ginger

Melt butter and golden syrup in large pan over a low heat. Add bicarbonate of soda mixed with boiling water.

Combine dry ingredients in a mixing bowl, then pour melted mixture into centre and mix to a moist but firm consistency.

Drop slightly rounded teaspoonful of mixture on to cold greased tray. Cook for about 15 minutes in a moderate oven. Cool on a wire rack.

Drover's damper

Traditionally made by bushmen, damper can be cooked in the hot ashes of a fire. The outside will be burnt; the damper is broken open and only the centre eaten. This is a sophisticated version of the basic recipe. It is excellent with pumpkin soup.

2 cups self-raising flour
½ teaspoon salt
2 teaspoons sugar
1 tablespoon butter
1 cup milk

Sift flour and salt. Add the sugar. Rub in butter. Mix in milk to make medium soft dough. Knead lightly on board until smooth. Pat into round shape. Place in tin and glaze with milk. Bake in hot oven, reducing heat until cooked (20 minutes). Turn out on to tea towel, wrap and cool. Serve with butter and golden syrup (cocky's joy) or jam.

Variations: to make fruit or grated cheese damper use 1 cup of either ingredient, added to basic recipe. Beer damper can be made by substituting beer instead of milk.

English is spoken in many places but the Australian brand is unmistakable. To the British our 'G'day, mate' will be curious, to the American it will be delightful and to a home-sick Aussie it will be music to the ears.

Here is a guide to some of the most common Aussie expressions and their meanings.

ace—excellent

'angon—wait a moment

arvo—afternoon

'avago—have a go (usually 'ya mug'—you fool—is added); try harder

barbie—short for barbecue

bewdy or bewdy bottler—good; the best

beyond the Black Stump—far from the city; the outback

bingle—minor car accident

bombed out—unsuccessful; *also* drunk

bushed—lost; *also* tired

by crikey—an expression of surprise

cark it—to die

cashed up—having plenty of ready money

cheesed (off)—bored; fed up

chewy—chewing gum

chook—a domestic fowl

chook raffle—a lottery in which the prize is a chicken; usually held in a 'pub' (hotel)

chuck a willy—go berserk

cobber—friend

cobberdobber—a person who informs on a friend

cocky—know-all (like cocky on the biscuit tin); *also* a small farmer

come a gutser (cropper)—to fall heavily

cot case—a drunk or exhausted person, fit only for bed

deadhead—a stupid person

dead marine—an empty beer bottle

dead set—certain; assured; used as an exclamation meaning 'really!'

dead set against it—unco-operative

dinky-di—genuine

do a Norm—to act foolishly

do the lolly (melon; nana; loaf)—to get very angry

dob in—to betray or report someone to the authorities; *also* to nominate someone for an unpleasant task

don't get off your bike—calm down

doughy—stupid

drongo—stupid person

dunny—an outside toilet

esky—a portable icebox (brand name)

fair crack of the whip—ease up

fair dinkum—honest; genuine

fair enough—all right; acceptable

fair go—a chance; *also* an appeal for fairness

five-finger discount—shoplifting

flake (out)—to collapse; to fall asleep

flat out like a lizard drinking—lying prone; *also* rushed, extremely busy

flush—having plenty of money

fossick—to search for something

DID YOU KNOW?
Sir Donald Bradman made his first century at the age of twelve at Bowral High School.

freak out—to have an extreme reaction (good or bad) to something

full as a goog (tick; boot)—drunk

garbage!—an exclamation meaning 'what rubbish, I don't believe you!'

go off like a bucket of prawns in the sun—to create a commotion

good one—an exclamation of approval

gutful—more than enough

have tickets on oneself—to be conceited

hit the deck—to duck; to put one's head down

hit the tin—to put money in the kitty; to contribute to a collection of cash

hoon—a stupid or uncultivated person

hooroo—goodbye

jigging—playing truant from school

kick in—to help out with money

knock—to criticise, find fault

knocker—a person who makes derogatory remarks

like a hornet in a bottle—furious

like a possum up a gum tree—moving fast

like a rat up a drainpipe—moving even faster

lingo—language

loaded—extremely wealthy; *also* very drunk

mate—good or best friend; *also* used to greet someone as in 'G'day mate'

matilda—a blanket roll carried by a swagman

m'oath—my oath, on my oath

mug—a fool; *also* face

mulga—rough country

no-hoper—an incompetent person; a social misfit

nosh-up—a good meal

nick—to steal

nick off—to go away; expression meaning 'lose yourself!'

get nicked—to be caught

nifty—stylish; clever; shrewd to the point of dishonesty

ocker—the archetypal uncultivated Australian man

'ooroo—goodbye

outback—the inland country far away from the cities

prang—minor car accident

rack off—to go away; expression meaning 'lose yourself!'

ring-in—a substitute

sangers—sandwiches

scungies—swimsuit worn for surfboard riding

shonky—poor quality; shoddy

skip—Australian-born (from Skippy the Kangaroo)

skite—a bragger

stinker—an objectionable person

stone the crows—exclamation of astonishment

swag—a blanket roll of light bedding

swagman—a man who travels around the country on foot and takes odd jobs

ratbag—a rogue; an eccentric person

rubbish—to criticise; to mock

ta ta!—bye bye!

take a sickie—to take a day off work

tax—to steal; to nick

tinnie—a can of beer

too right—an exclamation meaning 'I quite agree'

top drop—a good beer

true blue—genuine

twit—a fool

up-ta-putty—terrible

vegie—a silly person

veg-out—to do something foolish

wag it—to play truant

wheelie—a noisy skidding turn while driving

whinge—to complain

whopper—something surprisingly big

wowser—a killjoy; a prudish teetotaller

write-off—a total loss

yakka—hard or heavy work

yobbo—a stupid or uncultivated person

zonked (out)—tired out; exhausted

DID YOU KNOW?

The first point in Australia which is touched by the morning sun is Mount Warning near Murwillumbah in New South Wales, and the last touching point in the evening is Dirk Hartog Island near Exmouth in Western Australia.

Acknowledgments

This book has evolved from many sources and I wish to sincerely thank the many people who helped me gather material. I also wish to thank my friends and family, particularly my husband, without whose constant encouragement and vigilance the book would not have become a reality.

I would also like to thank the staffs of the following organisations: Antarctic Division, Kingston, Tasmania; Australian Bureau of Statistics; Australian Information Service; ANZ Bank; Department of Aboriginal Affairs; Department of Agriculture; Department of Immigration; Department of Foreign Affairs; Bureau of Meteorology; Cricket Association of Australia; Institute of Aboriginal Studies; Main Roads Department, New South Wales; the Mitchell Library, New South Wales; New South Wales Government Information Service; Peat, Marwick, Mitchell & Co; Pier 1 Hornsby Bookshop, Sydney; Reserve Bank; Sports Womens Association; State Tourist Commissions in each state; the Honours Secretariat; the Premier's Department in each state; the Department of the Prime Minister and Cabinet; the State Protocol Departments; Water Resources Commission; and the libraries of the Sydney Opera House, Hornsby Shire Council, Main Roads Board, New South Wales; Sport's Resources Centre, New South Wales; Mr Ray Mitchell; and the Maritime Services Board.

Finally, for permission to include copyright material I wish to thank Angus & Robertson Ltd for 'Waltzing Matilda' and 'The Man from Snowy River', from *The Collected Verse of A B Paterson* © Retusa Ltd; Mimmo Cozzolino for symbols reproduced from his book *Symbols of Australia*; the Department of the Special Minister of State for the Commonwealth flag and coat-of-arms; the Department of the Premier and Cabinet in Victoria, South Australia and Western Australia, the Premier's Department in New South Wales, Queensland and Tasmania, and the Department of the Chief Minister in the Northern Territory for the state flags and coats-of-arms; Kraft Foods Ltd for the Vegemite label; The Mitchell Library for the engraving 'The Settlement at Sydney Cove 1788'; the National Art Gallery of Victoria for 'The Rabbiters' by Russell Drysdale, and 'Shearing the Lambs' and 'The Sunny South' by Tom Roberts; and 'Landing of Captain Cook at Botany Bay 1770' by E Phillips Fox; the National Library of Australia for the engravings 'Sturt's party threatened by blacks . . .' by J Macfarlane and 'Attempted escape of prisoners from Darlinghurst Gaol' from *Illustrated Sydney News* 1864; the Government Printer, Sydney, for the engraving 'Arrival of the first railway train at Parramatta, from Sydney'; Sydney Opera House Trust for the photograph of Joan Sutherland in *The Merry Widow*; WEA Records for the photograph of Mental as Anything. Permission to reproduce the poem 'My Country' by Dorothea Mackellar was granted by the copyright holders, c/- Curtis Brown (Aust) Pty Ltd, Sydney. Kath Walker for her poem 'Then and Now'.

Every effort has been made to trace ownership of copyright material used in this book but apologies are made where any omission has occurred.

List of sources

The author acknowledges her indebtedness to the following books, which were consulted for reference.

Title	Author/Editor	Publisher	Year
Ampol's Sporting Records	John Blanch	Jack Pollard	1973
Australia: Colonies to Commonwealth 1850–1900	K M Adams	A & R	1971
Australia, The Greatest Island	R Raymond and Morrison	Lansdowne	1981
Australia Since Federation	Fred Alexander	Nelson	1980
Australian Aborigines	Norman Tindale and B George	Lloyd O'Neill	1983
Australian Encyclopaedia	John Shaw	Collins	1984
Australian Encyclopaedia of Rock	Noel McGrath	Outback Press	1978
Australian Political Institutions	Don Aitken and Brian Jinks	Pitman	1985
Australian Sporting Hall of Fame	Mike Gibson and Ian Chappell	A & R	1984
Australian Wildlife 1984	Elaine Russell	Bay Books	1983
Australians in the Antarctic	Australian News and Information Bureau		1961
Australia's Natural Wonders	Michael Richardson and Robin Newman	Golden Press	1984
Australia's Yesterdays		Reader's Digest	1974
Background Notes 1981	Department of Aboriginal Affairs		1981
Bold Atlas of Australia, The	J Roberts	Ashton Scholastic	1984

Title	Author	Publisher	Year
Complete Book of Australian Mammals	Australian Museum	A & R	1983
Encyclopaedia of Australian Sport	Jim Shepherd	Rigby	1980
Early Colonial Society	Carolyn Rasmussen	Nelson	1984
Focus on Government	D L Wallace et al	Pitman	1979
Great Geographical Atlas, The	Mitchell Beazel	Rigby	1984
I See No End to Travelling	Ann Millar	Bay Books	1986
Last New Wave, The	David Stratton	A & R	1980
Macquarie Book of Events, The	Bryce Fraser	Macquarie Library	1983
Macquarie Dictionary, The	Arthur Delbridge	Macquarie Library	1981
Merit Student's Encyclopaedia		Macmillan	1978
One Thousand Famous Australians		Rigby	1978
Pictorial Atlas of Australia, The		Rigby	1977
Restless Years, The	Peter O'Shaughnessy	Jacaranda	1968
Short History of Australia, A	Manning Clark	Macmillan	1981
Sunburnt Country, A	B Beavan and H Bogdan	Rigby	1978
What Bird is That?	N W Cayley	A & R	1973
Who's Who in Australia	W J Draper	Herald	1984

Demographic statistics are the estimated resident population for local government areas at June 1986, compiled by the Australian Bureau of Statistics.

A census is taken every five years and the results of the 1986 census are due in September 1987.

Facts and figures on the economy are from the Australian Bureau of Statistics 1985 and 1986 Year Books and the 1985 and 1986 Year Books of the individual states.